Mind Mechanics™ for Children

Mind Mechanics™ for Children

A Mental Health Toolbox with
Activities and Lesson Plans for Ages 7–11

SARAH RAWSTHORN

Jessica Kingsley Publishers
London and Philadelphia

First published in Great Britain in 2021 by Jessica Kingsley Publishers
An Hachette Company

1

A CIP catalogue record for this title is available from the British Library and the Library of Congress

ISBN 978 1 78775 713 4
eISBN 978 1 78775 714 1

Printed and bound in Great Britain by CPI Group UK

Jessica Kingsley Publishers' policy is to use papers that are natural, renewable and recyclable products and made from wood grown in sustainable forests. The logging and manufacturing processes are expected to conform to the environmental regulations of the country of origin.

Jessica Kingsley Publishers
Carmelite House
50 Victoria Embankment
London EC4Y 0DZ

www.jkp.com

This book is dedicated to Clive and India, my family and my friends, all of whom have inspired and supported me unfailingly, in my mission to make hard times in young lives more manageable, by providing toolboxes for brainboxes.

Acknowledgements

I am indebted to a number of people who have supported Edge Inclusion Partners in developing and evaluating this programme, especially Emma Short B.A. MBACP, Rita McKinnon, Elizabeth Banks, Carol Rayner, the Cheshire Community Foundation, Dr Sam Todd, Jeanie Davies, Tamsyn Marceau Magee and all at The Rooms, Middle Table and House Creative.

I would like to express gratitude for the work of Professor Paul Gilbert, Dr Martin Seligman and Dr Rebecca Duckhouse.

Finally, I'd like to thank the staff, students and families at Broken Cross Primary Academy and Fallibroome Academy in Cheshire for enabling me to pioneer this specially crafted mental health care programme with their students.

Contents

PART ONE

An Introduction to Mind Mechanics™

CHAPTER ONE

Why Teach about Mental Health and Emotional Wellbeing Issues?

It is shocking to learn that suicide has now replaced accidents as the biggest killer of teenagers and those aged under 25.

It is becoming apparent to everyone that mental health is as important a part of life as physical health and we need to learn and teach how to protect our mental health. Physical education lessons are often compulsory in schools because we view physical health as something our children need to learn about. We teach them about eating healthily and staying fit. Pre-school children know that if they have a cut a plaster will protect them; they understand that they should brush their teeth and wash their hands. We all have physical health. Sometimes we are well and healthy, sometimes we have poor physical health. We try our best to protect our physical health but what about our mental health?

As with physical health, there are actions that we can take to keep ourselves mentally well. However, children are not routinely taught to understand mental health, nor how to manage and protect themselves. Poor mental health is something that everyone deals with at some point in their life, perhaps seeking help with mental illness, helping someone else, or simply dealing with stressful and challenging times and situations.

As educators we need to portray mental health as crucial and equally important as physical health (because it is) – and that starts with making mental health education available.

Mental health education helps to keep the children and young people in our schools safe and enables them to better access the educational opportunities we make available to them, to achieve to the best of their ability so that they are better equipped for life: 'Teaching wellbeing in schools will improve the lives of young people and drive up test results'.[1] Additionally, talking openly with children and young people about mental health issues is a simple and effective means of breaking down any possible associated stigma.

---

1   www.tes.com/news/martin-seligman-teaching-wellbeing-schools-will-improve-lives-young-people-and-drive-test

Teaching about mental health and emotional wellbeing may raise significant challenges for teachers, however. We know that schools want to cover these issues and recognise the imperative to do so, but without sufficient knowledge and teaching resources, teachers may find it daunting. Mind Mechanics™ is the solution.

CHAPTER TWO

Introducing Mind Mechanics™

Who, How and What?

This book is aimed primarily at education and mental health professionals working with children of the chronological or developmental age of 7 to 11. Although we think that a range of people who work with children, young people and their families will find it a very useful tool, a professional background in education, child development, psychology or mental health is advantageous.

The full Mind Mechanics™ programme consists of a series of lesson plans with over 15 hours of evidence-based, high-impact activities and photocopiable/downloadable resources.

This Mind Mechanics™ book can be used very flexibly, in any of the following ways:

- **As a universal whole school scheme of work:** The Mind Mechanics™ programme can be used in its entirety as the scheme of work for Mental Health Education as a key part of your setting's Personal Social, Health and Citizenship or Social and Emotional Learning curriculum: a universal teaching resource for all students. The programme in Part Two is arranged into six workshops, including an introductory workshop, followed by five themed workshops that each contain approximately two hours of content, as follows: 1) Introducing Mind Mechanics™ to Participants – Including Pre-Intervention Assessment; 2) Emotions; 3) Calming Techniques and Liking Yourself; 4) Resilience and Self-Soothing; 5) Identifying Signature Strengths; 6) Using Signature Strengths and Support Networks and Post-Intervention Assessment. Each two-hour workshop can be split into shorter activities, over a number of different sessions if needed, permitting maximum flexibility in use.

- **As a targeted intervention for a group or individual:** The programme can be used as a targeted resource for those children identified as being vulnerable or with a diagnosed mental health condition. You may wish to select particular activities to create a bespoke mental health curriculum or intervention to meet specific need.

- **As a resource bank of individual activities:** To aid you in selecting particular activities to use as and when you choose, suggested timings for each activity are given in the content outline at the start of the workshop plans, and those activities most suited to being used individually are denoted with an asterisk.

Please note that once the introductory session has been covered, it is *not* imperative to complete the themed activities in order *nor* to adhere to the advisory time limits; these are simply for guidance and will depend on the number of participants.

ASSESSMENT AND IMPACT

The programme includes an introductory session, assessing both the children's prior knowledge and skills in the field of mental health and taking a snapshot of the mental health of individual participants through standardised assessment tools.

The final workshop recaps on learning and assesses progress using the same assessment tools post-intervention. By using the pre- and post-intervention assessment tools at your first and last sessions, you will be able to measure the progress of individual children and use these assessments to target further intervention, or evidence need, when making referrals to specialist mental health services.

For further information with regard to the efficacy of the programme and how you will be able to use these tools to evidence impact in your setting, please see Appendix: Impact Data and Case Study.

For those children who developmentally are emotionally skilled and literate, you may wish to consider using the *Mind Mechanics™ for Teens and Young Adults* book from the *Mind Mechanics™ for Mental Health* series to extend their skills and knowledge.

RESOURCES

All resources required are listed and should be readily available in school. Many resources are created by the participating students as part of the activity plans, and templates and photocopiable sheets are included. The photocopiable resources are also available to download from https://library.jkp.com/redeem using the code CMTVFUL. Every child should make or be provided with a homemade cardboard toolbox (or commercially sold mini toolbox) that they can keep their resources from each week's workshop in to use as and when they need them during the day.

WHAT IS MIND MECHANICS™?

Mind Mechanics™ is a mental health education programme developed through collaboration between our specialist teachers, psychologists and counsellors, each bringing expertise, a breadth and depth of professional knowledge and passion for change. The skills, strategies and understanding necessary to maintain good mental health are delivered through classroom-based activities designed to facilitate better understanding and self-regulation of emotions. This will help to reduce mental health problems and teach strategies to better manage or protect against existing poor mental health. The result will be an improvement in life chances for participants, reducing escalation of need and demand on specialist providers.

AIMS OF MIND MECHANICS™

- to teach participants to understand brain function in relation to emotional regulation and mental health

- to enable participants to better manage their ability to cope with difficult times and emotions

- to enable participants to better support others with their emotional wellbeing and mental health

- to reduce stigma around mental health.

KEY LEARNING OBJECTIVES

- to understand the concept of mental health

- to develop vocabulary and understanding of mental health conditions

- to explore self-perception

- to introduce resilience – risk and protective factors; personality, family and social

- to better identify what emotions we and others have and how we show them

- to develop an understanding of the reptilian and limbic brain in terms of the emotional regulation system, the threat detection-protection system, the drive-wanting-excitement system and the soothing-contentment-caring system

- to develop skills of mindfulness

- to learn relaxation techniques

- to express emotion through creativity

- to identify unhelpful/unhealthy soothing strategies

- to identify helpful/healthy soothing strategies

- to introduce and explain self-talk – learning to develop compassionate self-talk

- to identify an individual's strengths

- to share and explore the meaning of these strengths and how to utilise them

- to explore sympathy and empathy

- to develop the concept of self-management of emotional wellbeing

- to identify who is in our support network and how to find other sources of support

- to work on turn taking

- to develop group cohesion.

WHAT SETS MIND MECHANICS™ APART?

The Mind Mechanics™ programme will build capacity within your team. It provides upskilling through delivery, pre- and post-assessment, and teaching resources.

We welcome additional, broader mental health training with the aim of giving practitioners the skills to identify signs of mental health issues in young people and guide them to a place of support. However, we feel that raising awareness of definitions of poor mental health and signposting support services is not enough: it does not enable school personnel to provide intervention and support for students. Mind Mechanics™ addresses the gap in existing resources by providing a holistic package to draw upon in a bespoke way.

CHAPTER THREE

Prerequisites to the Programme

WORKING WITH PARENTS/CARERS

Evidence shows that if parents/carers can be supported to better manage their children's mental health, alongside work being carried out with the child at school, there is a much greater likelihood of success in reducing the child's problems, and in supporting their academic and emotional development.

However, while it is good practice to involve parents/carers and families wherever possible, in some circumstances the child or young person may wish not to have their parents/carers involved with any interventions or therapies they are receiving. In these cases, schools should be aware that those aged 16 or over are entitled to consent to their own treatment, and their parents/carers cannot overrule this. Children under the age of 16 can consent to their own treatment if it is thought that they have enough intelligence, competence and understanding to fully appreciate what is involved in their treatment. Otherwise, someone with parental responsibility can consent for them.

Students are far more likely to seek support for their mental health concerns following a workshop on a topic that is relevant to any current concerns they are facing and where they have developed the knowledge and confidence to seek help.

Also, there may be issues within the cohort you intend to teach which you are not aware of, but which are known about by other members of staff. By informing relevant pastoral or safeguarding staff and staff who lead on mental health issues of your intended topics, you can help them to prepare vulnerable students for your workshop.

CLASSROOM GROUND RULES

When teaching areas of the curriculum such as mental health, it is important to think carefully about the possibility of personal disclosures from students who, as a result of the workshop, may develop the skills, language, knowledge and understanding to make a disclosure about their own mental health or emotional wellbeing. While this is not to be discouraged, and appropriate disclosures should be seen as a positive impact of the learning, it is very important that if students make personal disclosures to school staff they do so in a suitable one-to-one setting. It is not appropriate to encourage students to talk about sensitive personal matters in the classroom.

Before teaching about mental health issues and emotional wellbeing, clear 'ground rules' should be established or reinforced, and the concepts of confidentiality and anonymity should be covered at the start of the workshop. Ground rules need to be consistently kept to, regularly revisited and, if necessary, renegotiated and reinforced.

The teacher should lead the way by modelling the ground rules in their own communications with the class. Ground rules are most effective when they have been negotiated and agreed with the students, rather than imposed by the teacher.

Teachers tell us that the most effective ground rules are:

- written in students' own words

- visually displayed in the classroom

- physically signed by students in some cases (like an informal contract)

- monitored by students themselves

- kept to consistently by the teacher as well as the students.

Below are some areas to explore with your class. These may arise naturally during negotiation; if not, you may want to consider introducing them.

Openness

An important part of breaking down the stigma that surrounds mental health issues is to encourage an ethos of openness, but within specific boundaries. These should be governed by your school's safeguarding policy. Mental health should not be a taboo topic. It should be openly and honestly discussed in the classroom setting, which should feel like a safe and supportive environment for discussions on mental health that are positive and affirming but give students the opportunity to share their concerns. However, it needs to be agreed with students that workshop time is not the appropriate setting to directly discuss their own personal experiences or the private lives of others. General situations can be used as examples, but names and identifying descriptions should be left out.

Keep the conversation in the room. Students need to feel safe discussing general issues related to mental health in the workshop without fear that these discussions will be repeated by teachers or students beyond this setting.

Students should feel confident exploring their misconceptions or questions about mental health in this safe setting. But it is important to make it clear that if you become concerned that a child may be at risk then you will need to follow the school's safeguarding policy, and that you personally cannot completely guarantee that no other student will repeat what has been said outside the classroom.

Non-judgemental approach

When we tackle issues surrounding mental health and emotional wellbeing, we often find that students have a lot of existing beliefs, misunderstandings and inappropriate attitudes towards the topics concerned. It is important that these can be explored within the classroom environment without fear of being judged or ridiculed. Discuss with students the idea that it is okay – and often healthy – to disagree with another person's point of view, but it is never okay to judge, make fun of or put down other students. Where students disagree with another's point of view, they should challenge the belief and not the person.

Right to pass

Although participation in the workshop is important, every student has the right to choose not to answer a question, or not to participate in an activity. Students may choose to pass on taking part if a topic touches on personal issues which they should not disclose in a classroom setting, or if the topic of the activity or discussion makes them feel uncomfortable in any way. They could be invited to discuss their concerns with the teacher individually.

Teachers can prepare the class by letting them know the nature of the topic beforehand and offering students the opportunity to let the teacher know, either anonymously or directly, if they have any concerns about themselves or a friend. This will enable you to ensure that your teaching is as inclusive as possible and is matched to the students' needs.

Make no assumptions

In addition to not judging the viewpoints of others, students must also take care not to make assumptions about the attitudes, life experiences, faith values, cultural values or feelings of their peers.

Listen to others

Every student in the class has the right to feel listened to, and they should respect the right of their peers to feel listened to as well. You might choose to revisit what actively listening to others means. It is okay to challenge the viewpoint of another student, but we should always listen to their point of view, in full, before making assumptions or formulating a response.

Use of language

Students should be reminded to take care in their use of language in (and beyond) workshops about mental health. They should not be using vocabulary that is inaccurate or offensive.

There are many words surrounding mental health that have negative connotations or may be misunderstood by students. It can be valuable to explore these words and understand exactly why they are inappropriate and should not be used either in the setting of a workshop, or in day-to-day life. You might, for example, consider with students how they would feel if such words were applied to them. These include 'nutter' and 'loony bin' or the use of 'mental' or 'crazy' in a derogatory fashion.

Students should also be reminded not to use words or phrases that trivialise mental health issues. This would include phrases like 'That's so OCD!' or telling people with significant issues to 'pull themselves together' or keep their 'chin up'.

There are a lot of commonly used phrases that trivialise mental health issues, and students often use them without meaning to cause harm. Taking the time to consider how such phrases might be perceived by someone who was facing anxiety, depression or other mental health issues can help to address their use of such language both within and beyond the PSHE classroom.

You might suggest the following ground rules: 'We will use the correct terms for the things we will be discussing rather than the slang terms as they may be offensive. If we are not sure what the correct term is, we will ask our teacher.' 'We will not use language that might be perceived as trivialising mental health issues.'

Ask questions

It is important to foster an open environment where students feel safe asking questions and exploring their preconceptions about a topic. Students should understand that no question will be considered stupid, and that when they are in doubt about an issue or topic, they should ask. It is also important that students realise it is never appropriate to ask a question in order to deliberately try to embarrass somebody else or to encourage students to laugh at someone.

Making an anonymous question box available to students can be an effective way of enabling them to ask questions they may feel uncomfortable about posing in a classroom setting. You can make this available before, during or after the workshop. You will need to allow yourself time to go through and read the questions.

Inviting questions prior to the workshop can be a good way to help you direct the workshop during its development, based on the current needs and understanding of your class, and can also give a good indicator of any safeguarding issues or pastoral issues which need to be followed up.

Seeking help and advice

Students should be actively encouraged to seek support or advice if they have concerns about themselves or a friend, either during or following a workshop.

IMPLEMENTING SAFEGUARDS TO ENSURE THE WELLBEING OF VULNERABLE STUDENTS

Even if you don't know of any current issues amongst the students in the class you'll be teaching, prepare all workshops on the basis that there will be at least one member of the class who is personally affected by the workshop content. Think carefully about how to make the workshop safe for that student; this will help to ensure the workshop is safe for everyone.

Safeguards you can put in place include:

- alerting relevant pastoral and safeguarding staff about the topic you'll be covering and encouraging them to discuss the workshop content with any students who are accessing support for related issues

- clearly signposting sources of support before, during and after the workshop

- taking care to avoid the use of images, language or content which may prove distressing or a trigger to vulnerable students

- when using case studies, taking care to ensure they are completely unlike any members of your class – where possible, use names which are different to those of your students, and situations which do not reflect the current or past experiences of any students in the class.

While sometimes there may be clear physical or emotional indicators that a student is vulnerable to the issues we're discussing in class, sometimes there will be no such indicators at all. Some young people work very hard to keep their problems hidden, so we must work hard to make our workshops universally safe and never make assumptions about the wellbeing or resilience of particular students.

SIGNPOSTING SUPPORT

Although it is important that students do not make personal disclosures during the course of the workshop, the appropriate means for seeking support and advice need to be clearly signposted in the workshop. This will mean being familiar with, and sharing appropriate parts of, the school's safeguarding or other relevant policies. You should be aware of any internal support available in the school, such as counselling services or pastoral care, and be able to explain to students how to access that support.

For the best mental health practice, we recommend that schools should consider appointing a lead contact or coordinator for mental health issues, and if your school does adopt this model, you will want to work with them on advice to students about accessing support. You should also share details of relevant external websites and helplines where students can seek confidential advice and support. In addition, students should be encouraged to support their friends in seeking help where they think it is needed.

While clarifying that during a workshop is not the appropriate moment to seek support, you should ensure that students understand the importance of sharing with a trusted adult any concerns they have about their own mental health or emotional wellbeing, or that of another person. This is the quickest and best way to ensure that support is received where it is needed.

Students should be reassured that they will always be taken seriously, will never be judged and will always be listened to if they choose to make a disclosure at school. It is important not only to signpost sources of support but also to make sure students know how to access it, both in terms of the practical mechanisms and, especially with younger students, what they might say to someone to get the help they need.

Make sure you are fully aware of the policies and procedures you should follow if a student confides in you or gives you cause for concern. It is important not to promise confidentiality if information is disclosed which suggests a child is at risk. If policies are not fit for purpose or procedures are out of date or unclear, this should be highlighted with the relevant member of staff.

PREPARING OR WITHDRAWING VULNERABLE STUDENTS

If you are aware of students in your class who are likely to find the topic of the workshop particularly sensitive, perhaps due to their own pre-existing mental health condition or that of a family member, then the workshop content should be discussed with them beforehand. This may be done by an adult specifically involved in their care and wellbeing, for example a form tutor or school counsellor. The student must have the right to withdraw from the workshop, and in such cases they should not be expected to justify their absence to their peers. If the workshop is missed, then consideration should be taken as to how to follow up the missed workshop with the student in question so that they are able to benefit from the learning, as the outcomes of the workshop may be especially relevant to them.

CHAPTER FOUR

Risk and Resilience

Mind Mechanics™ is designed to equip participants to respond to stress in a healthy way. An important part of managing challenge is having a resilient approach. Resilience means the strength to overcome or bounce back from difficult experiences. Research has proven that encouraging the development of skills and aptitudes related to resilience can support students and make them less vulnerable to external stressors present in their environment.

Research has uncovered a number of factors which have been found to promote better outcomes for children and young people who have faced adversity. Some findings relate to biologically determined internal factors which cannot be altered. However, there are a range of other, both internal and external, factors which have been found to enhance children and young people's chances of overcoming adversity.

An important mechanism through which schools promote resilience is allowing students to experience meaningful success. As Daniel Goleman (who many credit with bringing awareness of the importance of emotional intelligence to popular attention) says, people who are in anxious, angry or depressed states are unable to learn; the working memory is effectively swamped.[1]

Resilient students are more likely to engage with other people, adults and peers alike. They have good communication and problem-solving skills, including the ability to recruit substitute caregivers; they have a talent or hobby that is valued by their elders and peers; and they have faith that their own actions can make a positive difference in their lives. By fostering resilience in all our students, we are equipping them with the necessary skills for a successful transition into adulthood.

Certain individuals and groups are more at risk of developing mental health problems than others. These risks can relate to the child themselves, to their family, or to their community or life events. The risk factors are listed in Figure 4.1.

---

1 Goleman, D. (1995) *Emotional Intelligence*. New York, NY: Bantam Books.

Risk factors		**Protective factors**
• Difficult temperament • Low self-esteem • Negative thinking style	**Child**	• Easy temperament • Good social and emotional skills • Optimistic coping style
• Family disharmony, instability or breakup • Harsh or inconsistent discipline style • Parent(s) with mental illness or substance abuse	**Family**	• Family harmony and stability • Supportive parenting • Strong family values
• Peer rejection • School failure • Poor connection to school	**School**	• Positive school climate that enhances belonging and connectedness
• Difficult school transition • Death of family member • Emotional trauma	**Life events**	• Involvement with caring adult • Support at critical times
• Discrimination • Isolation • Socioeconomic disadvantage • Lack of access to support services	**Social**	• Participation in community networks • Access to support services • Economic security • Strong cultural identity and pride

Figure 4.1 Mental health: Risk factors and protective factors

Risk factors are cumulative. Students exposed to multiple risks such as social disadvantage, family adversity and cognitive or attention problems are much more likely to develop behavioural problems. Longitudinal analysis of data for 16,000 students suggested that boys with five or more risk factors were almost 11 times more likely to develop conduct disorder under the age of ten than boys with no risk factors. Girls of a similar age with five or more risk factors were 19 times more likely to develop the disorder than those with no risk factors.[2]

Schools offer important opportunities to prevent mental health problems by promoting resilience; providing students with inner resources that they can draw on as a buffer when negative or stressful things happen helps them to thrive even in the face of significant challenges. This is especially true for children who come from home backgrounds and neighbourhoods that offer little support. In these cases, the intervention of the school can be the turning point. Having a 'sense of connectedness' or belonging to a school is a recognised protective factor for mental health.

---

2   Murray, J.J. (2010) 'Very early predictors of conduct problems and crime: Results from a national cohort study.' *Journal of Child Psychology & Psychiatry 51*, 11, 1198–1207.

CHAPTER FIVE

Mental Health Statistics and Impact Factors

MENTAL HEALTH STATISTICS

Of children and young people aged 5–16, 9.8 per cent have a clinically diagnosed mental disorder.[1]

Within this group, 5.8 per cent of all children have a conduct disorder (this is about twice as common among boys as girls), 3.7 per cent have emotional disorders, 1.5 per cent have hyperkinetic disorders and a further 1.3 per cent have other less common disorders including autism spectrum disorder, tic disorders, eating disorders and mutism. Out of all children, 1.9 per cent (approximately one fifth of those with a clinically diagnosed mental disorder) are diagnosed with more than one of the main categories of mental disorder. Beyond the 10 per cent discussed above, approximately a further 15 per cent have less severe problems that put them at increased risk of developing mental health problems in the future.[2]

GOOD MENTAL HEALTH

Children who are mentally healthy have the ability to:

- develop psychologically, emotionally, intellectually and spiritually

- initiate, develop and sustain mutually satisfying personal relationships

- use and enjoy solitude

- become aware of others and empathise with them

- play and learn

---

1 https://digital.nhs.uk/data-and-information/publications/statistical/mental-health-of-children-and-young-peoplein-england/2017/2017
2 ibid.

- develop a sense of right and wrong

- resolve (face) problems and setbacks and learn from them.

FACTORS IMPACTING ON YOUNG PEOPLE'S EMOTIONAL WELLBEING

To be able to provide relevant information and support to our students, it's vital that we understand the pressures they are currently under.

A recent survey from Place2Be for Children's Mental Health Week found that two-thirds of primary school children say they worry all the time about at least one thing to do with their home life or school life.

Young Minds, a UK charity which provides information and support about young people's mental health issues, found that the following issues were the key factors causing concern to school-aged children.

Fear of failure

Children and young people are expressing fear of failure at increasingly younger ages. Many schools report an increase in emotional wellbeing issues as some students prepare to take school entrance exams, or where there is an emphasis on success in tests. It is very common for schools to report an increase in issues as students approach major examinations as well. High expectations are often internally driven by students themselves in addition to any external pressure which may be present from parents or the school.

Bullying

Bullying is a key trigger for mental health and emotional wellbeing issues, as well as being a key maintaining factor (that is, children who are attempting to overcome difficulties find it far harder to do so in a context of teasing and bullying). Bullying can be face to face or online – and in many cases both. It's important to understand that sometimes what is meant in good humour or jest is very easily misinterpreted or can escalate rapidly, causing distress and emotional pain to vulnerable students.

Body image

Body image is a real concern amongst all young people – not just young women as is often believed – and low self-esteem and poor body image are a leading cause of students opting out of extracurricular activities or failing to engage in class. The pressure to look a certain way or weigh a certain amount is felt keenly by many students, regardless of their gender, and these pressures can contribute to the development of eating disordered behaviour as well as a range of other emotionally and physically harmful responses.

The online environment

Students may see little or virtually no division between the online and offline world. They may have many friends who they know purely in an online context and they do not see this as problematic or unusual. Much of what we teach in an offline context with regard to developing healthy relationships and staying safe can be readily adapted to address the online context too. Potential dangers to students online include abuse and grooming, cyberbullying and becoming involved in dangerous communities which advocate harmful behaviours (for example 'pro-ana' communities, which advocate anorexia as a lifestyle choice and provide advice and support to maintain this 'lifestyle' as opposed to promoting support to change these harmful behaviours).

Sexual pressures

Ready access to pornography has led to an increase in the sexual pressures felt by the current generation of children and young adults. Young people talk about pressures to look and behave a certain way when in a relationship, as they are used to viewing the way that people look and behave in pornography. This access to pornography may also be one factor contributing to an increase in abuse in teenage relationships, as it often portrays relationships where consent is neither given nor sought.

COMMON TRIGGERS FOR UNHEALTHY RESPONSES

There is not always a clear cause or trigger for mental health or emotional wellbeing issues. But it is certainly true that children and young people are more likely to develop issues such as anxiety or depression, or harmful behaviours such as self-harm or alcohol or drug misuse, at times of particular stress. It is worth being aware of these trigger points so that we can increase our prevention through early intervention efforts around these times, and keep an eye on students who may be more vulnerable to developing issues than their peers due to their current circumstances. Common triggers for unhealthy responses in school-aged children include the following.

Family relationship difficulties

Difficulties at home can take a huge toll on a young person's emotional wellbeing. The difficulties may be between the parents or may concern the young person directly, such as a difficult falling out with a family member. Stable family relationships are a fantastic source of emotional support for young people, so it's important to think about where that support is coming from, and what extra support might be needed when things are difficult at home.

Peer relationship difficulties

Similarly, difficult relationships at school can leave children feeling desperate and with no one to turn to. In these instances, they are far more likely to turn to unhealthy coping mechanisms such as self-harm, disordered eating or substance abuse.

Trauma

Experiencing trauma – for example a bereavement, being involved in an accident or suffering abuse – will leave a child very vulnerable and in huge need of support. It is important to bear in mind that this is about the student's perception of trauma, not our own, so difficulties may be triggered by something seemingly insignificant but which has had a deep impact on the child or young person concerned, such as the death of a pet.

Being exposed to unhealthy coping mechanisms in other students or the media

When young people are exposed to self-harm, eating disorders or other unhealthy coping mechanisms, either by witnessing them first-hand or by watching them on TV or the internet, they are more likely to replicate such behaviours themselves. Teachers should be especially vigilant and respond proactively if popular or high-profile programmes watched by a large number of students run stories involving eating disorders or self-harm.

Difficult times of year

The anniversary of a significant event such as the death of a parent is often a very difficult time for a young person. It is sensible to keep a note of any such dates on their files as it is not uncommon for problems to arise seemingly out of the blue many years after the trauma as a student marks a milestone anniversary or if they are also contending with other difficulties (e.g. exam stress). An anniversary or birthday of a lost loved one can be the final straw which renders them unable to cope. This is an example of when good communication between class teachers/form tutors, pastoral leads and Personal, Social and Health teachers (if they are not one and the same person) are so important.

Exam pressure

The pressure of tests and exams is keenly felt by students and is a very common trigger for mental health problems. Teachers should be keeping an extra close eye on children as they enter periods of exams and also during times when academic pressure increases significantly.

Transition to a new school

Transition to a new school can be very difficult for children and young people, who may miss the familiarity of their old setting and may need to establish new friendship groups. This is true of students who are making the natural progression 'up to big school' even if they are accompanied by some of their friends, and is even more acute for children who move schools part way through a school year due to a family move or following a permanent exclusion, for example.

Illness in the family

If a parent or sibling falls seriously ill, this can put a huge pressure on a young person, who is likely to take on some form of caring role while inevitably receiving less time and attention from loved ones due to the focus on the family member who is unwell. They may also be harbouring deep worries about the wellbeing of their relative. In this situation, young people often feel unable to voice their worries or concerns for fear of being a burden and may instead turn to other coping mechanisms such as alcohol, drugs or self-harm.

VULNERABLE GROUPS

Some young people are more vulnerable than their peers to developing mental health or emotional wellbeing issues. These include: children in care, children who have been adopted, LGBTQ+ students, children whose family have a history of mental health issues, young carers and young offenders.

CHAPTER SIX

Disorders Defined and Appropriate Intervention

The UK Department for Education Mental Health and Behaviour in Schools guidance defines the most common mental health disorders and describes the most appropriate evidence-based interventions for depression, anxiety and conduct disorders. Mind Mechanics™ takes the format of small group work based on focusing on the knowledge, skills and understanding described for each area of need.

CONDUCT DISORDERS (E.G. DEFIANCE, AGGRESSION, ANTI-SOCIAL BEHAVIOUR, STEALING AND FIRE-SETTING)

Overt behaviour problems often pose the greatest concern for practitioners and parents/carers, because of the level of disruption that can be created in the home, school and community. These problems may manifest themselves as verbal or physical aggression, defiance or anti-social behaviour. In the clinical field, depending on the severity and intensity of the behaviours they may be categorised as oppositional defiant disorder (ODD – a pattern of behavioural problems characterised chiefly by tantrums and defiance which are largely confined to family, school and peer group) or conduct disorder (CD – a persistent pattern of anti-social behaviour which extends into the community and involves serious violation of rules). According to the World Health Organization, 10 per cent of the child and adolescent population may experience behaviour problems.[1] Many children with attention deficit hyperactivity disorder (ADHD) will also exhibit behaviour problems. Such problems are the most common reason for referral to mental health services for boys, and the earlier the problems start, the more serious the outcome. There is, however, evidence to support the effectiveness of early intervention.

The strongest evidence supports prevention/early intervention approaches that include a focus on: the whole school environment, particularly addressing bullying; and teaching social and emotional skills and small group sessions for children with a focus

---

1 World Health Organization (WHO) (2001) 'Mental health: New understanding, new hope.' Geneva: World Health Organization. Available from: www.who.int/whr/2001/en/whr01_en.pdf?ua=1

on developing cognitive skills and positive social behaviour and staff training as part of a multisystem intervention.

ANXIETY

Anxiety problems can significantly affect a child's ability to develop, to learn or to maintain and sustain friendships. Children and young people may feel anxious for a number of reasons – for example because of worries about things that are happening at home or school, or because of a traumatic event. Symptoms of anxiety include feeling fearful or panicky, breathless, tense, fidgety, sick, irritable, tearful or having difficulty sleeping. If they become persistent or exaggerated, then specialist help and support will be required. Clinical professionals make reference to a number of diagnostic categories:

- generalised anxiety disorder (GAD) – a long-term condition which causes people to feel anxious about a wide range of situations and issues, rather than one specific event

- panic disorder – a condition in which people have recurring and regular panic attacks, often for no obvious reason

- obsessive-compulsive disorder (OCD) – a mental health condition where a person has obsessive thoughts (unwanted, unpleasant thoughts, images or urges that repeatedly enter their mind, causing them anxiety) and compulsions (repetitive behaviour or mental acts that they feel they must carry out to try to prevent an obsession coming true)

- specific phobias – the excessive fear of an object or a situation, to the extent that it causes an anxious response, such as panic attack (e.g. school phobia)

- separation anxiety disorder (SAD) – worry about being away from home or about being far away from parents/carers, at a level that is much more than normal for the child's age

- social phobia – intense fear of social or performance situations

- agoraphobia – a fear of being in situations where escape might be difficult, or help wouldn't be available if things went wrong.

While the majority of referrals to specialist services are made for difficulties and behaviours which are more immediately apparent and more disruptive (externalising difficulties), there are increasing levels of concern about the problems facing more withdrawn and anxious children, given the likelihood of poor outcomes in later life.

The strongest evidence supports prevention/early intervention approaches that include a focus on regular targeted work with small groups of children exhibiting early signs of anxiety, to develop problem solving and other skills associated with a cognitive behavioural approach.

DEPRESSION

Feeling low or sad is a common feeling for children and adults, and a normal reaction to experiences that are stressful or upsetting. When these feelings dominate and interfere with a person's life, it can become an illness. According to the Royal College of Psychiatrists, depression affects 2 per cent of children under 12 years old, and 5 per cent of teenagers. Depression can significantly affect a child's ability to develop, to learn or to maintain and sustain friendships. There is some degree of overlap between depression and other problems. For example, around 10–17 per cent of children who are depressed are also likely to exhibit behaviour problems.[2] Clinicians making a diagnosis of depression will generally use the categories major depressive disorder (MDD – where the person will show a number of depressive symptoms to the extent that they impair work, social or personal functioning) or dysthymic disorder (DD – less severe than MDD, but characterised by a daily depressed mood for at least two years).

The strongest evidence supports prevention/early intervention approaches that include a focus on regular work with small groups of children concentrating on cognition and behaviour – for example changing thinking patterns and developing problem-solving skills – to relieve and prevent depressive symptoms.

HYPERKINETIC DISORDERS (E.G. DISTURBANCE OF ACTIVITY AND ATTENTION)

Although many children are inattentive, easily distracted or impulsive, in some children these behaviours are exaggerated and persistent, compared with other children of a similar age and stage of development. When these behaviours interfere with a child's family and social functioning and with progress at school, they become a matter for professional concern. Attention deficit hyperactivity disorder (ADHD) is a diagnosis used by clinicians. It involves three characteristic types of behaviour – inattention, hyperactivity and impulsivity. Whereas some children show signs of all three types of behaviour (this is called 'combined type' ADHD), other children diagnosed show signs only of inattention or hyperactivity/impulsiveness.

Hyperkinetic disorder is another diagnosis used by clinicians. It is a more restrictive diagnosis but is broadly similar to severe combined type ADHD, in that signs of inattention, hyperactivity and impulsiveness must all be present. These core symptoms must also have been present before the age of seven and must be evident in two or more settings.

The strongest evidence supports the following:

- Medication should be used where ADHD is diagnosed and other reasons for the behaviour have been excluded. These treatments have few side effects and are effective in 75 per cent of cases when there is no depression or anxiety accompanying ADHD. High doses can be avoided if behavioural treatments accompany medication.

---

2 Tyler, C. (2018) 'Keynote Speech.' NAHT and RCOP Joint Conference: Education and Mental Health. London. 30 January 2018.

- Where there is insufficient response to medication, parent education programmes and individual therapy should be introduced. These need to be provided in the school as well as at home, as they do not appear to generalise across settings.

- For children also experiencing anxiety, behavioural interventions may be considered alongside medication.

- For children also presenting with behavioural problems (e.g. conduct disorder, Tourette's syndrome, social communication disorders), appropriate psychosocial treatments may also be considered by medical professionals.

Evidence also supports:

- making advice about how to teach children with ADHD-like behaviour in their first two years of schooling widely available to teachers and encouraging them to use this advice.

ATTACHMENT DISORDERS

Attachment is the affectionate bond children have with special people in their lives that lead them to feel pleasure when they interact with them and be comforted by their nearness during times of stress. Researchers generally agree that there are four main factors that influence attachment security: opportunity to establish a close relationship with a primary caregiver; the quality of caregiving; the child's characteristics; and the family context. Secure attachment is an important protective factor for mental health later in childhood, while attachment insecurity is widely recognised as a risk factor for the development of behaviour problems.

The strongest evidence supports:

- video feedback-based interventions with the mothers of pre-school children with attachment problems, with a focus on enhancing maternal sensitivity.

Evidence also supports:

- the use of approaches which employ play as the basis for developing more positive child–parent relationships.

EATING DISORDERS

The most common eating disorders are anorexia nervosa and bulimia nervosa. Eating disorders can emerge when worries about weight begin to dominate a person's life. Someone with anorexia nervosa worries persistently about being fat and eats very little. They lose a lot of weight and if female, their periods may stop. Someone with bulimia nervosa also worries persistently about weight. They alternate between eating very little and binging. They vomit or take laxatives to control their weight. Both of these eating disorders affect girls and boys but are more common in girls.

The strongest evidence supports the following:

- The primary aim of intervention is restoration of weight and in many cases inpatient treatment might be necessary.

- For young people with anorexia nervosa, therapeutic work with the family – taking either a structural systemic or behavioural approach – may be helpful even when there is family conflict.

- For young people with bulimia nervosa, individual therapeutic work focusing on cognition and behaviour, for example to change thinking patterns and responses, may be beneficial.

Evidence also supports the following:

- Early intervention is necessary because of the significant risk of ill-health and even death among sufferers of anorexia.

- School-based peer support groups used as a preventative measure (i.e. before any disordered eating patterns become evident) may help improve body esteem and self-esteem.

- When family interventions are impracticable, cognitive-behavioural therapy (CBT) may be effective.

SUBSTANCE MISUSE

Substance misuse can result in physical or emotional harm. It can lead to problems in relationships at home and at work. In the clinical field, a distinction is made between substance abuse (where use leads to personal harm) and substance dependence (where there is a compulsive pattern of use that takes precedence over other activities). It is important to distinguish between young people who are experimenting with substances and fall into problems, and young people who are at high risk of long-term dependency. This first group will benefit from a brief, recovery-oriented programme focusing on cognitions and behaviour to prevent them to move into more serious use. The second group will require ongoing support and assessment, with careful consideration of other concurrent mental health issues.

The strongest evidence supports the following:

- Therapeutic approaches which involve the family rather than just the individual assist communication, problem solving, becoming drug-free and planning for relapse prevention. These approaches are especially helpful with low-level substance users, and when combined with CBT or treatments focusing on motivation.

- Where families cannot be engaged in treatment, a variation of family therapy known as 'one-person family therapy' can be used.

- Multi-Systemic Therapy, Multi-Dimensional Family Therapy, the Adolescent Community Reinforcement Approach and other similar approaches (which consider wider factors such as school and peer group) can be used where substance misuse is more severe and part of a wider pattern of problems.

Evidence also supports:

- the introduction of programmes as a preventative measure – delivered in community settings or schools and focusing on developing skills that enhance resilience – as substance abuse is connected to other problems that can be addressed within these settings.

DELIBERATE SELF-HARM

Common examples of deliberate self-harm include 'overdosing' (self-poisoning), hitting, cutting or burning oneself, pulling hair or picking skin, or self-strangulation. The clinical definition includes attempted suicide, though some argue that self-harm only includes actions which are not intended to be fatal. It can also include taking illegal drugs and excessive amounts of alcohol.

It can be a coping mechanism, a way of inflicting punishment on oneself and a way of validating the self or influencing others.

The strongest evidence supports:

- brief interventions engaging the child and involving the family, following a suicide attempt by a child or young person

- assessment of the child for psychological disturbance or mental health problems which, if present, should be treated as appropriate (at times, brief hospitalisation may be necessary)

- some individual psychodynamic therapies (Mentalisation Based Treatment) and behavioural treatments (Dialectic Behaviour Therapy).

POST-TRAUMATIC STRESS

If a child experiences or witnesses something deeply shocking or disturbing, they may have a traumatic stress reaction. This is a normal way of dealing with shocking events and it may affect the way the child thinks, feels and behaves. If these symptoms and behaviours persist, and the child is unable to come to terms with what has happened, then clinicians may make a diagnosis of post-traumatic stress disorder (PTSD).

The strongest evidence supports:

- therapeutic support focused on the trauma and which addresses cognition and behaviour especially regarding sexual trauma. Some can be delivered in schools, such as trauma and grief component therapy and cognitive behavioural intervention for trauma in schools (CBITS). Trauma-focused CBT should be adapted appropriately to suit age, circumstances and level of development.

The evidence specifically does not support:

- prescription of drug treatments for children and young people with PTSD

- the routine practice of 'debriefing' immediately following a trauma.

PART TWO

Mind Mechanics™ Workshop Plans, Activities and Resources

Those activities most suited to being used as standalone activities for intervention/ teaching activities are denoted by an asterisk. All references to the downloadable/ photocopiable resources appear in bold.

Introducing Mind Mechanics™ to Participants – Including Pre-Intervention Assessment

1. Key Learning Objectives, Resources and Teaching Input Overview

2. Introduction, Content and Purpose (5 minutes)

3. Rules and Safety (10 minutes)

4. Assessment – Pre-Intervention (15 minutes)

5. My Goals (10 minutes)

6. All about Me Collage (40 minutes) and Group Share (15 minutes)*

7. Social Network Constellation (10 minutes)*

8. Closing Activity (10 minutes)

KEY LEARNING OBJECTIVES

- To understand the purpose of Mind Mechanics™

- To be introduced to the content of the workshops

- To devise rules and discuss safety

- To begin to develop group cohesion

- To explore self-perception

- To become aware of individual social networks

RESOURCES

- A3 paper, pens, glitter, old magazines, papers, craft material, fabric scraps, stickers

- Scissors

- Flip chart and pen

- Files/homemade cardboard toolboxes (as appropriate to age and stage)

- Sticky labels

- Pre-Intervention Assessment Tools: **Emoji Assessment Tool, How Are Things? Assessment Tool** and **Me and My Life Assessment Tool**

- **My Goals** sheet

- **Social Network Constellation** worksheet

TEACHING INPUT OVERVIEW

1. Introduce the purpose and content of Mind Mechanics™.

2. Develop a list of five agreed rules for use during the programme.

3. Complete the pre-intervention assessment tools – outcome and wellbeing measures.

4. Define what individual participants wish to achieve.

5. Create an All about Me Collage – build in achievements and identify self-perceived strengths.

6. Group Share.

7. Complete a Social Network Constellation.

8. Closing Activity – physical tasks.

Introduction, Content and Purpose (5 minutes)

Resources

- Files/homemade cardboard toolboxes (as appropriate to age and stage)

- Sticky labels

Ask students if they have any ideas about what 'Mind Mechanics™' might be about and take responses.

> *The Mind Mechanics™ workshop is where we will learn about how our brains work and train ourselves to use the strengths we have and develop new strategies to help us stay mentally healthy. So we'll be using our experiences, our imagination and problem-solving skills to look at emotions, thoughts and behaviours and how we can control and change them to keep us the best we can be.*
>
> *It's called Mind Mechanics™ because we are all going to become the mechanics of our own mind.*
>
> *We will learn about how to help ourselves with our emotions and behaviours and change things in lots of fun ways. We will make different tools to help us calm down, stop worrying, feel good and get better at things using our strengths. These will be our toolboxes [present toolboxes to children] that we put all our tools and strategies in, and at the end of the programme you can take your toolboxes with you, with everything you've made to help you at home and at school when you need them. You will all get a certificate at the end, once you have become a Mind Mechanic; then you can help yourself and help others whenever there is a difficult situation or you feel sad, worried, scared or angry, because you'll know lots of different things that can help and you'll have your toolbox. Does anyone have any questions?*

Ask students to use a sticky label and write their name using colours/stickers etc. (2–3 minutes) and stick it to their toolbox.

Rules and Safety (10 minutes)

Resources

- Flip chart and pen

Create ground rules with the group and write them on the flip chart. Please see Chapter 1 for guidance around devising rules. Adapt suggestions from the children in line with school policy and confidentiality. Allow a maximum of five rules from the group, adding that there are no right or wrong answers and they may opt out of sharing exercises whenever they wish – they can input as much or as little as they feel comfortable with.

Assessment – Pre-Intervention (15 minutes)

Resources

- **Emoji Assessment Tool**

- **How are Things? Assessment Tool**

- **Me and My Life Assessment Tool**

- Pens/pencils

Assessment tools will be completed on the first and last sessions of the programme to see if things have helped or if any more help is needed. Emphasise that the tools are *not* a test and wherever the children rate themselves is okay. Ask the children to be as honest as they can with each question. Tell them that their answers will be confidential and will not be shared with others unless they choose to share. Talk through each question (where necessary) and address any questions that arise.

Resource: Emoji Assessment Tool

PRE-INTERVENTION	
POST-INTERVENTION	

Have a look at the following expressions and think about which ones you can relate to at the moment. Put a tick in the boxes for the ones which best describe how you are generally feeling. You can choose one, or as many as you like.

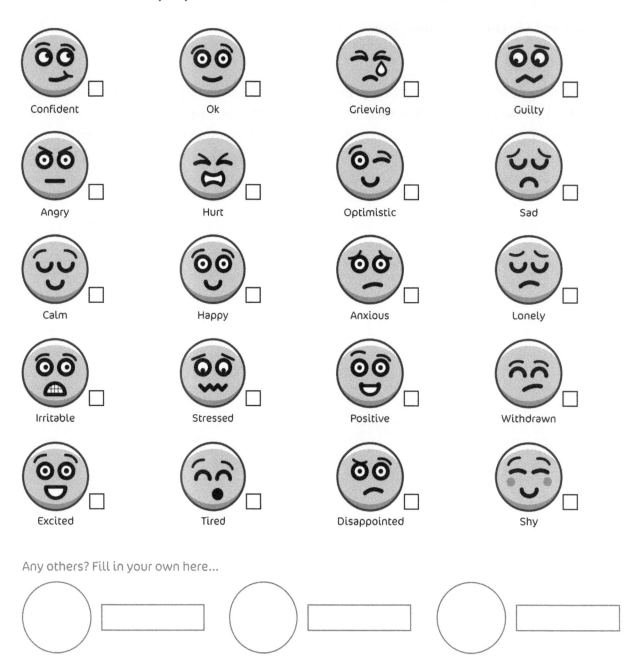

Confident ☐ Ok ☐ Grieving ☐ Guilty ☐

Angry ☐ Hurt ☐ Optimistic ☐ Sad ☐

Calm ☐ Happy ☐ Anxious ☐ Lonely ☐

Irritable ☐ Stressed ☐ Positive ☐ Withdrawn ☐

Excited ☐ Tired ☐ Disappointed ☐ Shy ☐

Any others? Fill in your own here...

Resource: How Are Things? Assessment Tool

Below is a table that asks how you have been feeling over the past week. You should just pick the number which is the best match for you. There is no right or wrong answer.

Over the last week...		None of the time	Rarely	Some of the time	Often	All of the time
1.	I've felt anxious	1	2	3	4	5
2.	I felt like being on my own	1	2	3	4	5
3.	I've felt able to deal with my problems	1	2	3	4	5
4.	I've thought of injuring myself	1	2	3	4	5
5.	I have thought that I could ask someone to help if I've been worried or unhappy	1	2	3	4	5
6.	My thoughts and feelings have upset me	1	2	3	4	5
7.	My problems have been too much too handle	1	2	3	4	5
8.	I've been sleeping badly	1	2	3	4	5
9.	I've felt down	1	2	3	4	5
10.	I've been able to do the things I've wanted to do	1	2	3	4	5

Below is a questionnaire which is going to ask you how you feel. There are no right or wrong answers. You should just pick the answer which is best for you. For example, the statement might be 'I feel happy' and then you will have to decide how often you feel happy – 'Never', 'Sometimes' or 'Always' – and then mark that option.

		0	1	2
1.	I get very cross	Never	Sometimes	Always
2.	I lose control	Never	Sometimes	Always
3.	I lash out when I am upset	Never	Sometimes	Always
4.	I cause harm to people	Never	Sometimes	Always
5.	I am chilled out	Never	Sometimes	Always
6.	I destroy things intentionally	Never	Sometimes	Always
7.	I am mean to others	Never	Sometimes	Always

Date: . . . . / . . . . / . . . .   Time: . . . .

Now give yourself 2 points for Always, 1 point for Sometimes and 0 points for Never. Add up your total. You may use pre- and post-assessment scores to measure progress and to identify unmet development needs.

Total: . . . .

Resource: Me and My Life Assessment Tool

For each statement put a mark where you are on the chart.

0 = low/not very much

10 = high/very much

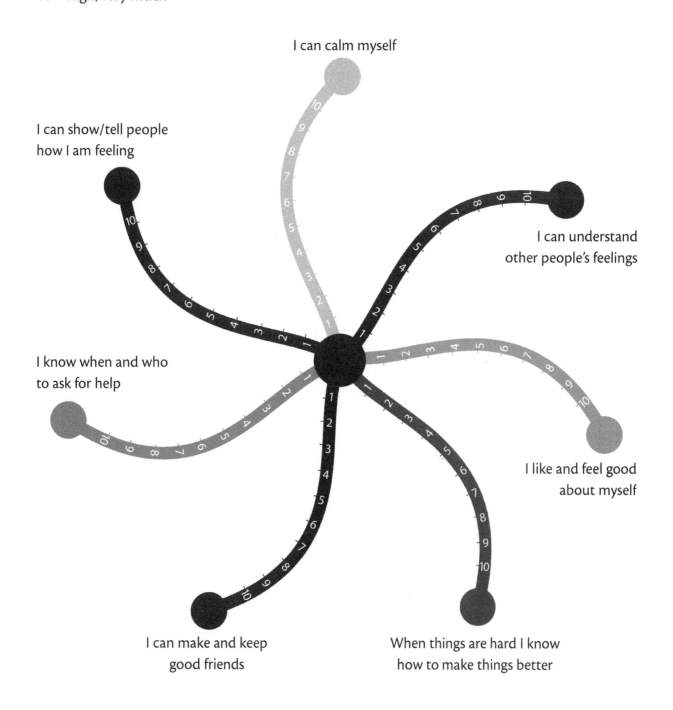

I can calm myself

I can show/tell people how I am feeling

I can understand other people's feelings

I know when and who to ask for help

I like and feel good about myself

I can make and keep good friends

When things are hard I know how to make things better

My Goals (10 minutes)

Resources

- **My Goals** sheets
- Pens/pencils

Ask students to write down any goals or a goal that they would like to achieve during the workshops focusing on emotional wellbeing, learning and behaviour. These goals are confidential unless they wish to share them with others. Prompts might include: learn to be calmer, control anger, learn about the brain, what to do when they can't sleep when they are worried, coping with a relationship. Tell them we will be rating how close to our goals we get each workshop.

Resource: My Goals

Name:
Goal 1:
Goal 2:
Goal 3:

For each of your goals think about how you are doing in achieving it, then circle the number in the table

0 = not achieved my goal in any way

5 = halfway to achieving my goal

10 = fully achieved my goal

Week	Goal 1:										
1	0	1	2	3	4	5	6	7	8	9	10
2	0	1	2	3	4	5	6	7	8	9	10
3	0	1	2	3	4	5	6	7	8	9	10
4	0	1	2	3	4	5	6	7	8	9	10
5	0	1	2	3	4	5	6	7	8	9	10
6	0	1	2	3	4	5	6	7	8	9	10

Week	Goal 2:										
1	0	1	2	3	4	5	6	7	8	9	10
2	0	1	2	3	4	5	6	7	8	9	10
3	0	1	2	3	4	5	6	7	8	9	10
4	0	1	2	3	4	5	6	7	8	9	10
5	0	1	2	3	4	5	6	7	8	9	10
6	0	1	2	3	4	5	6	7	8	9	10

Week	Goal 3:										
1	0	1	2	3	4	5	6	7	8	9	10
2	0	1	2	3	4	5	6	7	8	9	10
3	0	1	2	3	4	5	6	7	8	9	10
4	0	1	2	3	4	5	6	7	8	9	10
5	0	1	2	3	4	5	6	7	8	9	10
6	0	1	2	3	4	5	6	7	8	9	10

All about Me Collage and Group Share (55 minutes)

Resources

- A3 paper
- Pens
- Glitter
- Old magazines

- Papers
- Craft material
- Scissors
- Blank stickers/sticky notes

Collage (40 minutes)

Invite students to create a collage from the magazines and other resources provided, to be shared with the group. The collage is to be all about them. It can include anything and everything, including how they feel about life, what they like and dislike, or things that excite or worry them in the world.

Lay out the blank stickers/sticky notes as students finish their collage and ask them to write any strengths or achievements on these and add them to the front or back of their collage.

Group Share (15 minutes)

In sharing their collages invite each child to talk about their work by starting with 'My name is… and…'. Notice things about their work as they share, such as the presence of certain pictures or colours. For example, say, 'You chose this picture because…' or 'I notice you used lots of glitter on your picture,' allowing them to respond if they wish. Reflect back a summary as accurately as possible at the end of each student's sharing.

Never give a personal opinion of their work or say what you like about it. If you want to draw something out of the picture that resonates with you, own the response and begin with something like, 'When I see the colours on your picture it makes me feel…' or 'I feel a sense of…when I look at…'.

Ask if there are any words to describe themselves and also any strengths or achievements they identified. Repeat their name and their word or strength(s)/achievement(s) (if they give any) or thank them, using their name.

Social Network Constellation (10 minutes)

Resources

- **Social Network Constellation** worksheet per student

- Pens/pencils

Introduce the Social Network Constellation as a way of establishing the positive relationships and connections the children have in their life, and those around them who are important to them. Give examples of the people they may put in each section (they may want to include pets): people who love me (family/carers); people who like me (friends and neighbours); people who are paid to know and help me (named personnel at school/clubs).

Resource: Social Network Constellation

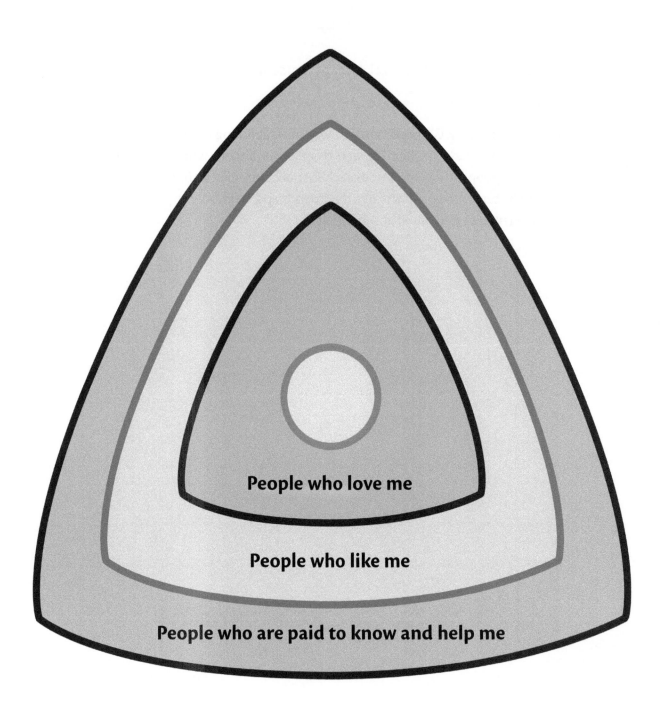

People who love me

People who like me

People who are paid to know and help me

Closing Activity (10 minutes)

The following activity can be done as many times as you have time for at the end of the session, each task becoming harder than the last.

Ask the students to form a line side by side in order of:

- where their first name falls alphabetically (for younger students give direction about where they should begin, for example A–Z from left to right)

- their birthday (for younger students the month or date number)

- beginning letter of their road or street name

- shoe size (without speaking)

- height (with eyes closed).

Theme One: Emotions

1. Key Learning Objectives, Resources and Teaching Input Overview

2. Warm Up: The Sitting Challenge and Discussion (10 minutes)*

3. Recap Rules and Workshop 1 Content (5 minutes)

4. Body Scanning and Lion Emotions (30 minutes)*

5. Emotion Labelling (10 minutes)*

6. Emotion Role Play and Movement (55 minutes)*

7. Focusing on Feeling: Back to Back Drawing and Discussion (19 minutes)*

KEY LEARNING OBJECTIVES

- To better identify what emotions we and others have and how we show them
- To identify sensations and feelings
- To learn about the old and new brain
- To develop an understanding of the concept of emotional regulation
- To begin to express emotion through creativity

RESOURCES

- A1/A2 paper
- Pens/pencils
- Highlighter pens
- Glue
- Scissors
- Flip chart paper
- **My Goals** sheet from Workshop 1
- Toolboxes
- Large sheet of paper/wallpaper roll
- Commercially available/homemade emotion cards (i.e. drawings or pictures of individual emotions such as *Love, Jealousy, Anger* written on separate cards) and envelopes labelled with the corresponding words
- Folders/clipboards to lean on
- **Lion Emotions Outline** worksheets
- **Lion Emotions Teacher Prompt** sheets
- **Back to Back Drawing 1, 2 and 3** sheets

TEACHING INPUT OVERVIEW

1. Warm Up: The Sitting Challenge and Discussion.

2. Recap Rules and Workshop 1 Content.

3. Body Scanning and Lion Emotions.

4. Labelling envelopes – when I am…(emotion) I…(behaviour).

5. Back to Back Drawing.

6. Discuss the challenge of expressing some things without saying what they are.

Warm Up: The Sitting Challenge and Discussion (10 minutes)

The Sitting Challenge (5 minutes)

Around a table, or in a circle, ask the students to begin by standing up. Explain that the goal of the challenge is for everyone to be sitting down at the end of one minute, but no two people must sit down at the same time. If this happens, everyone must stand and begin again. They must not communicate with anyone else in any way during the minute.

If the challenge is not completed on the first attempt, allow three more. If the challenge is completed first time, begin again giving 30 seconds. The total time to be spent on the task is three minutes.

During the task notice the engagement of the students and their responses to each other and the time limit. In the discussion to follow it will be helpful if you can bring your observations in to prompt the students in their reflection; for example, 'I noticed some people were hesitant in choosing to sit or stand and others sat very quickly. I wonder what you were feeling or thinking when you made your choices to sit? Where did you feel that in your body?'

The easiest way to complete this task is if the students realise they can sit down in order: once the student to their left sits down, they can sit down; and then the student to their right can sit down, and so on.

Discussion (5 minutes)

Ask the students what was difficult or easy about the task. Draw out that it is more difficult to know how others are thinking when it is not communicated verbally, but there are clues we can get from people's body language and non-verbal communication.

Ask them how they felt during the task, where they felt that or what it felt like in their bodies and whether they expressed that physically (through sound, e.g. a moan; a laugh/movement, e.g. pointing or clenching hands). Here are some examples that might come up:

- pressure or excitement because of the time limit

- frustration that they couldn't communicate with others

- boredom.

Recap Rules and Workshop 1 Content (5 minutes)

Can you remember all the group rules?

Recap on the agreed rules from last week and the importance of each one.

Can you remember anything about each other's collages or strengths from last week?

Ask each person their strengths.

Ask the students to look over their **My Goals** sheet and mark where they are on week 2. It might be the same as or different than last week.

Body Scanning and Lion Emotions (30 minutes)

Resources

- A1/A2 paper

- Coloured pens/pencils/crayons

- **Lion Emotions Outline** worksheets (one per pair)

- **Lion Emotions Teacher Prompt** sheets (one per pair)

Introduction (5 minutes)

Using a large piece of A1/A2 paper draw the outline of a person. Tell the students that in a short while they will be asked to draw on the figure any sensations they experience in their bodies when they feel 'happy', but that first we will do a quick experiment to use to help us to check what we are feeling.

Ask the students to imagine their mind is a laser scanner and they can scan their whole body for detection of any sensations. When they activate their body scan powers they can do it from head to toe going through all their muscles and organs like a scanning line, *or* they can operate like a sense radar allowing any sensation signals to be picked up whenever they happen and are detected by their brain.

Tell the children that they will be detecting where they feel happiness in their bodies. Invite them first to gently close their eyes and, without talking to anyone, to imagine a thing or things that make them really happy. Encourage them to imagine what they are doing and who they are with. Tell them to allow themselves to be filled full of that happy feeling.

Now tell them to activate their body scan. While they are holding the feeling of happiness they should check what each part of their body wants to do and whether there are sensations in their bodies: in their arms, hands, legs, tummies, and so on.

Body Scanning (10 minutes)

Ask the students, one at a time, to draw on the large figure where they feel a sensation in their body when they feel happy, using any colour they like. Demonstrate by drawing something on the **Lion Emotions Outline**, for example a warm feeling in the heart with red, or a big deep breath in the lungs with clouds of blue. Invite them to write any descriptive words around the outside of the figure.

Lion Emotions (10 minutes)

Ask the students to get into pairs and give each pair a **Lion Emotions Outline** worksheet. Assign an emotion to each pair from sad/anger/worried/scared and ask the students to work with their partner to write/draw all the sensations they feel when they experience that emotion onto the paper. Use the **Lion Emotions Teacher Prompt** sheet for inspiration if necessary.

Feedback (5 minutes)

Ask each pair to feed back to the group.

Resource: Lion Emotions Teacher Prompt

When I am happy *I think*...

life is amazing

this is so much fun

I love 'x'

When I am sad *I think*...

life is hard work

this is overwhelming

I hate 'x', etc.

When I am happy *I feel*...

tingly

like jumping on the settee

relaxed, warm, etc.

When I am sad *I feel*...

spiky

like hiding in my bed

flat, cold, etc.

Emotion Labelling (10 minutes)

Resources

- Emotion cards (commercial or homemade)

- Coloured envelopes

- Sheets of coloured paper

- Scissors

- Glue

- Pens/pencils

- **Lion Emotions Outline** sheet

The Emotion cards should be laid out and accessible, along with the **Lion Emotions Outline** sheet. Invite the students to do the following:

- They should choose a coloured envelope and piece of paper that represents 'happy' for them and write the word 'happy' on the front of the envelope.

- Next they need to choose an emotion card that represents how they are when they are happy and take it back to their seats.

- They should then copy the emotion word from their chosen emotion card in the middle of their coloured paper.

- Ask them to write on the **Lion Emotions Outline** sheet the things they do when they feel happy (behaviours), for example, 'I squeeze my hands and close my eyes', 'I run and hug my friend', 'I jump up and down'.

- At the top they should write the things they think when they are happy (thoughts), for example, 'I love this', 'I love being me', 'this is so exciting'. They should then add the envelopes with their pieces of paper to their toolbox.

Emotion Role Play and Movement (55 minutes)

Resources

- Emotion cards (one set per child)

- Sheets of coloured paper

- Coloured envelopes

- Pens

Invite the students to choose one of the following emotions: sad/worried/scared/angry, but not discuss it with anyone else. Ask them to return to the emotion cards choosing the one that best fits that emotion (without showing anyone) and return their 'happy' emotion card. They then return to their seats, placing the emotion card face down and then find a space in the room. Explain that in a moment they may act out their behaviour when they feel that emotion. (2 minutes)

Invite the students to move around the room, role playing what they do when they feel their chosen emotion. Ask them not to cross paths with others or make contact with anyone or anything in the room as they move around. After 1 minute shout 'Freeze!' and choose a child to role play their emotion around the other students. Ask the students to raise their hand to guess the emotion and say why they have chosen that answer. Allow each child a turn until everyone has told the others their emotion. For each child repeat what they are acting out: 'So A's emotion is...and when you feel this you... Is that right? And what might you be thinking?' Reflect on any similarities or differences with students who have chosen the same emotion. (10 minutes)

Ask the students to return to their seats and choose a coloured envelope and piece of paper for their chosen emotion (sad, worried, scared or angry). They should write their chosen emotion on the envelope, and the word from their chosen emotion card on the coloured paper.

- Say to the students that they may always act the same way when they feel X (emotion) or they may act differently in different places when they feel X.

- Invite them to reflect on whether they always act the same when they feel X.

- If not, they may add all the ways they act in each place (with the place name, for example 'school', 'home', etc. on their paper next to the relevant actions). They should use a different colour for each place. (10 minutes)

Repeat the bullet-pointed steps three times, returning the emotions cards each time until all the students have completed an envelope and piece of paper for each emotion. (7 minutes per emotion, 21 minutes total)

Focusing on Feeling: Back to Back Drawing and Discussion (19 minutes)

Resources

- Chairs
- Sheets of paper
- Pens/pencils
- Folders/clipboards to lean on
- Copies of the **Back to Back Drawings 1, 2 and 3** sheets

Back to Back Drawing (9 minutes)

Ask the children to get into pairs and to number themselves 1 or 2. Next they need to arrange their chairs so that their backs are against each other.

Give the 1s in each pair a copy of **Back to Back Drawing 1**. Give the 2s a piece of paper and a folder to lean on. (3 minutes to set up)

The 1 in each pair must now describe to the 2 where to draw on their paper to create the picture they are looking at using any instructions they wish. However, they must not tell or show the 2s what the drawing is. (3 minutes)

Repeat the exercise with the roles reversed, using **Back to Back Drawing 2** this time.

Once the 3 minutes are up, they may share their drawings with each other.

Discussion (5–10 minutes)

Allow each pair to show their drawings and feedback how they felt it went. Ask the students how this activity differed from the first activity – The Sitting Challenge and Discussion – when they weren't allowed to talk to each other. Discuss the challenge of expressing some things without saying what they are. Draw out how hard or easy they felt the task was and explore the reasons why.

Resource: Back to Back Drawing 1

Resource: Back to Back Drawing 3

Theme Two: Calming Techniques and Liking Yourself

1. Key Learning Objectives, Resources and Teaching Input Overview

2. Warm Up: The Key/Ring Keeper and Body Scanning (20 minutes)*

3. Recap Rules and Workshop 2 Content (5 minutes)

4. Soothing Breathing (10 minutes)*

5. Relaxation Exercises (20 minutes)*

6. Safe Place Imagery (15 minutes)*

7. Attention Placing (5 minutes)

8. Attention Cycle (10 minutes)

9. Memory Jars (30 minutes)*

KEY LEARNING OBJECTIVES

- To enable participants to develop the skill of mind training
- To introduce and explain self-talk – learning to develop compassionate self-talk
- To develop skills of mindfulness

RESOURCES

- A3/A4 paper and pastels/colouring pens/pencils
- A5 card sheets
- Toolboxes
- **My Goals** sheet from Workshop 1
- Rubber rings or beanbags
- Blindfold
- A 'breathing buddy'– a small cuddly toy/small world play figurine, etc.
- Coloured sand/salt (5–7 different colours)
- Plastic funnels, small plastic/glass jars with lids, trays
- **Relaxation Script**
- **The Place Guided Visualisation** Script
- **Attention Cycle** sheet
- **Mindfulness Script**

TEACHING INPUT OVERVIEW

1. Warm Up: The Key/Ring Keeper and Body Scanning.
2. Recap Rules and Workshop 2 Content.
3. Introducing mind training – through imagination and mentalisation, using:
   a. Soothing Breathing, using a 'breathing buddy' and relaxation exercises
   b. Safe Place Imagery
   c. Attention Placing (back of the head, toes, thumb)
   d. Relaxation
   e. Remembering safe and happy memories.

Warm Up: The Key/Ring Keeper and Body Scanning (20 minutes)

Resources

- Rubber rings or beanbags
- Blindfold

The Key/Ring Keeper (15 minutes)

The 'keeper' sits blindfolded in the centre of the room with five beanbags/rubber rings placed around them.

Other students stand around the edge of the room or in a larger circle away from the keeper.

The goal is for those on the outside to steal the bags/rings from the keeper by stealthily creeping and not getting pointed out by the keeper.

Explain the rules:

Students can only move when they are instructed to by the facilitator (you can do this by pointing at them). Once the person has set off they can then make a play for the keys. If the key keeper points at them, they have to return to their starting point, losing a life. They have two lives. The game will start off with one person at a time, before building up to several players attempting to retrieve the keys at once.

The keeper must use their sense of hearing to detect where the threat of those trying to steal the keys/rings is coming from. They may point to where they detect a threat. If they catch 'the threat' it is neutralised and you can select another student to attempt a steal. The keeper has two lives; if they identify a false threat they lose a life. Try to allow as many students as possible a chance as keeper.

While doing this exercise ask students to do a body scan at least twice to see what sensations they feel at different points and what emotion they are connected to.

Discussion (5 minutes)

Did anyone notice anything about their bodily sensations, emotions or actions during the game?

What were the keeper's feelings, having so many people around them and not being able to see?

What were the thief's feelings, wanting to get to the key but having to beat the keeper?

Recap Rules and Workshop 2 Content (5 minutes)

Resources

- Students' completed **My Goals** sheets from Workshop 1

- Pens/pencils

Go through the rules with the group, seeing if they can remember them.

Recap the Body Scan carried out in Workshop 2 and discuss how we think and act differently whenever we feel different emotions in different places.

This week we will be concentrating on the power of our mind, imagination and our senses and how we can use them to help us with a number of different calming techniques.

Ask students to look at their **My Goals** sheet and mark where they are on week 3. Again, it may be the same or different to last week.

Soothing Breathing (10 minutes)

Resources

- A 'breathing buddy'– a small cuddly toy/small world play figurine, etc. for each child

Ask the students if they notice any changes in the way they breathe when they feel sadness/anger/fear/worry and gather feedback. Talk about how breathing can increase and become shallow when we are upset because our mind is signalling to our body there is something wrong, and we are under threat even if the threat is only a thought and not a real thing.

Tell students that most of the techniques we learn, like 'body scanning', will require the power of our minds and senses but for this one we will use a helper: introduce the 'breathing buddy'.

Ask students to lie in a comfortable position on the floor. Then say:

Place the breathing buddy on the bottom of your belly. Our buddies will help us see how deep our breaths are – the higher the breathing buddy rises the deeper the breath. Imagine the breathing buddy is asleep and you want to keep a rhythm going to keep it sleeping. Take nice big, deep, slow breaths in. Gently hold your breath for a pause at the top and then breathe smoothly out again.

Relaxation Exercises (20 minutes)

Resources

- **Relaxation Script**

- Sheet of A5 card per student

- Pens/pencils

Tense and Relax Muscles (10 minutes)

Relaxation is like giving ourselves a mind massage.

Invite the students as a group to tense and release their muscles using the **Relaxation Script**.

Ask them to create an image of what the movement feels like as they do it, for example, scrunching their face and opening their eyes and mouth wide or shoulders scrunched and released out and down like a baker rolling dough out so it stretches.

Talk about how and when we might use this. For instance, we might combine it with soothing breathing for sleep or to help the adrenaline work its way out of the body when in the threat system.

Relaxation Routine (10 minutes)

Give each student a piece of A5 card which can be folded in half. Then say something along these lines:

> *Come up with a relaxation routine for one emotion. For example, if you were feeling sad or angry, which strategy would work best for you? What sort of breathing or relaxation exercise would you choose? Choose the emotion and begin writing your own routine.*

Resource: Relaxation Script

Begin by finding a comfortable position where you are sitting. Have your feet on the floor taking the weight of your legs, your back against the chair and the chair underneath you holding you.

Allow your attention to focus only on your body. If you notice your mind wandering, bring it back to what we are focusing on and the muscle we are concentrating on.

Take in a nice deep breath through your tummy, hold it for a few seconds, and breathe out slowly – making a noise if you want to, 'sighing' or 'blowing'. Take a few more breaths and notice your lungs filling with air as your stomach rises. With your breaths, imagine the tension flowing out of your body. Breathe at your own pace throughout this exercise, and tense and relax each muscle when you feel ready. We will do each area twice. In between just keep breathing naturally.

So we will start by curling your *toes* under, tensing your feet as you breathe in. Hold as your breath goes in and release as you breathe out. On your next breath in, repeat.

Now squeeze your *calves* and feel the muscles at the back of your legs at the bottom turn into balls of muscle as you breathe in. Hold as your breath goes in and release as you breathe out. On your next breath in, repeat.

Tighten your *thighs*, feeling the muscles in the top of your legs contract as you breathe in. Hold as your breath goes in and release as you breathe out. On your next breath in, repeat.

Tighten your *buttocks* under yourself and against the seat of the chair as you breathe in. Hold as your breath goes in and release as you breathe out. On your next breath in, repeat.

Gently arch your *lower back* as you breathe in. Hold as your breath goes in and release as you breathe out. On your next breath in, repeat.

Now tighten the *muscles in your stomach* by squeezing them together as you breathe in. Hold as your breath goes in and release as you breathe out. On your next breath in, repeat.

Tighten your *chest* by taking a deep breath in, hold for about 5 seconds, and breathe out, blowing out all the tension. Repeat.

Tense your *upper back* by making sure your shoulders push down and backwards as if they were trying to meet in the middle of your back as you breathe in. Hold as your breath goes in and release as you breathe out. On your next breath in, repeat.

Now lift your *shoulders* up as if they could touch your ears as you breathe in. Hold as your breath goes in and release as you breathe out. On your next breath in, repeat.

Move down your arms and flex your *biceps* as you breathe in. Hold as your breath goes in and release as you breathe out. On your next breath in, repeat.

Clench your *fists* tightly without straining as you breathe in. Hold as your breath goes in and release as you breathe out. On your next breath in, repeat.

Now moving to your head, tighten your *eye muscles* by scrunching your eyelids tightly shut as you breathe in. Hold as your breath goes in and release as you breathe out. On your next breath in, repeat.

Smile widely, feeling your *mouth and cheeks* tense up as you breathe in. Hold as your breath goes in and release as you breathe out. On your next breath in, repeat.

Lastly scrunch up the muscles in your *forehead* by raising your eyebrows as high as you can or frowning and scrunching up your nose as you breathe in. Hold as your breath goes in and release as you breathe out. On your next breath in, repeat.

Safe Place Imagery (15 minutes)

Resources

- Sheet of A4 paper for each child

- Pens/pencils

- **The Place Guided Visualisation**

Ask the students to sit comfortably, feet on floor, body on chair (FOFBOC) and listen intently for the next few minutes while they allow their imagination to take them on a trip. Ask them to either close their eyes or allow their eyes to look at the floor or keep their gaze low so they don't become distracted. Then read aloud **The Place Guided Visualisation**. (3 minutes)

At the end of the visualisation ask them to draw and colour onto their paper anything they imagined or what they feel now, telling them that this will be their safe place imagery. Ask them to write three lines on the back of the paper beginning 'I feel', one under the other, completing each sentence with something they are feeling. (10 minutes)

Then say something like:

When we feel soothed, we feel safe and loved, calm and able to be relaxed and open to other people and ourselves. We feel happy and able.

Discuss this with the children, linking the idea of a safe place to having a soothing system. (2 minutes)

Resource: The Place Guided Visualisation

This guided visualisation is to take you to a private place of your own that feels safe, secure and comfortable. A place you can return to in the future to help calm your mind and help you prepare for what you need to do.

Sit with a straight back, feet flat on the floor and your hands on your knees or resting on your belly – whatever feels right for you. Now take a lovely deep breath in and as you breathe out, let your eyes gently close or allow your gaze to fall to the floor so you can turn your attention inwards to your body and your imagination.

Breathe naturally and normally now as we continue.

I want you to imagine you are in a place. It can be anywhere – made up or real – but somewhere you feel happy and relaxed. Look around this place in your mind…

Is it inside or out?

What else is there with you?

What does it feel like – is it warm or cold, is there a breeze?

Are there any sounds in this place of yours?

Can you imagine any smells there that are soothing and familiar?

What else do you notice about the place?

Attention Placing (5 minutes)

Refer to the warm-up exercise The Key/Ring Keeper, and get feedback from those who were 'keeper' – where did they notice they had to place their attention? Ask those who were the takers of the key/rings where they placed their attention. Talk about attention being placed by choice away from other things which might distract it.

Invite the students to place their attention in the following places (allow 30 seconds before moving onto the next):

- *your right foot*

- *your left knee*

- *the back of your neck where your head meets your neck*

- *your left-hand middle finger.*

Take feedback.

Discuss how, when we are motivated, we focus on something and have the energy to finish it or achieve it – we are driven to win or complete something.

Attention Cycle (10 minutes)

Resources

- Copies of the **Attention Cycle** sheet (one per child)

- **Mindfulness Script**

This activity looks at motivation/drive and emotional regulation.

Go through the **Attention Cycle** sheet, discussing each stage with the students.

Then use the **Mindfulness Script** to take the children through the Attention Cycle exercise.

Resource: Attention Cycle

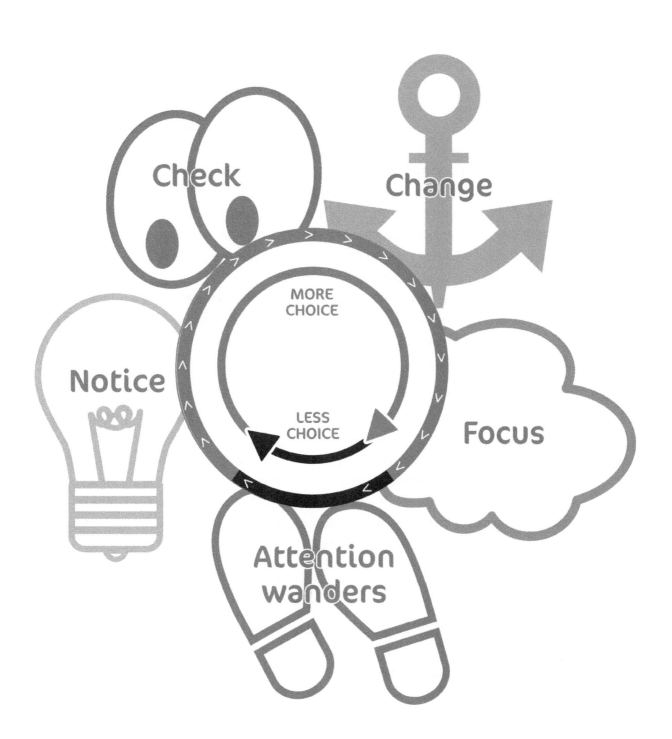

Resource: Mindfulness Script

It can be easy to rush through life without stopping to notice much.

Paying more attention to the present moment – to your own thoughts and feelings, and to the world around you – can improve how you feel in yourself. Some people call this 'mindfulness'. Mindfulness can help us enjoy life more and understand ourselves better. There are things you can do to use mindfulness in your own life.

Mindfulness is when we take some time to focus on **now**: when we really notice what our bodies are feeling and pay close attention to the things that are happening around us, no matter how small. It also helps us to see which of our thoughts are helpful and which aren't helpful and might be keeping us stuck. The Attention Cycle helps us to keep our attention on the thing we are doing when our mind wanders. By being mindful and going through the Attention Cycle we can move our thoughts and feelings away from unpleasant ideas and emotions.

Being mindful can also help us be much more aware of when we are feeling okay or not so okay, it helps us get back in touch with our bodies and start to notice more how our bodies are doing each day and what makes us feel good or not good.

Let's practise being mindful now.

1. FOCUS: Take a few moments to focus on your breathing. Close your eyes, get comfy and notice how fast or slow your breath is coming. Is it deep? Shallow? Smooth? Ragged? Is it easy to take a breath or does it feel like hard work? Are you breathing deep within your belly or is it your chest that is moving? Don't try to change anything. Just notice it. Move your attention outside of your body to what's around you. What can you hear? What is the temperature like? What can you smell? How does the place you are in make you feel? Can you notice the different things going on close by to you and then further away? What tiny sounds or movements are you aware of? Do you feel comfortable where you are right now?

2. ATTENTION: Is your mind wandering? This is natural, but bring it back to focusing on your breathing.

3. NOTICE: Next, check in with your body. Starting with the tips of your toes, focus all of your attention on each tiny body part. How do your toes feel? Do you know? Are they hot or cold? Do they tingle when you put your attention on them? Do you feel any sensations? Perhaps you don't feel anything? Notice it all! Then what about the bottoms of your feet? And your heels? What do you notice about how they feel? Work your way up your whole body like this and notice every tiny thing that you might be feeling.

4. CHECK, and if you need to, CHANGE: Notice what is going on in your mind. Is it quiet and still or is it buzzing with thoughts? Can you notice how your thoughts come and go? Is it easy to try to step away from them and simply notice them or do you find yourself quickly drawn back in?

Do your thoughts follow a pattern? Just watch for a little while and notice how your mind is working. Is there an image or a pattern that could describe it?

5. *Finally, FOCUS again: Take a moment to notice your breathing and your body once more. How do you feel now compared to when you started? You might feel the same or you might feel different. There is no right or wrong. Just notice.*

Being mindful isn't about going into it wanting a certain thing to happen or to feel a certain way. It's about tuning in to how you are feeling and the world around you.

You can practise at any time on your own.

Memory Jars (30 minutes)

Resources

- 7 different coloured sands/salts

- Funnels

- Trays

- Jars with lids (one for each student)

- Pens in the same colours as the coloured sand/salt

Ask the students to record at least seven happy memories that make them feel happy, safe, loved, lucky, all-round fantastic. Ask them to write the memories down, using a different colour for each memory.

Place the coloured sand/salt on the table with funnels. Give each student a sand bottle/jar.

Ask the students to work in pairs and tell them they are to go round the table together and talk about each memory as they fill their jar with their colourful memories. They can choose colours that they feel match their memories and can add more or less of one colour if they so choose. Ensure all jars are filled to the absolute maximum before putting the lids on so that the sand/salt doesn't move once sealed.

Workshop 4 Plan

Theme Three: Resilience and Self-Soothing

1. Key Learning Objectives, Resources and Teaching Input Overview

2. Warm Up: Parcel Wrap (15 minutes)*

3. Recap Rules and Workshop 3 Content (5 minutes)

4. Risk and Protective Factors (20 minutes)

5. Worry Box (10 minutes)*

6. Hug Tree (10 minutes)*

7. Identifying Emotions: Emotion Faces (10 minutes)*

8. Matching Emotions to Tools (47 minutes)

9. Role Playing Emotion Change (10 minutes)

10. Loop de Loop Teamwork (10 minutes)*

KEY LEARNING OBJECTIVES

- To introduce resilience – risk and protective factors; personality, family and social
- To identify unhelpful/unhealthy soothing strategies
- To develop ways of dealing with worry and negative thoughts

RESOURCES

- Empty shoe box/string/scissors/wrapping paper/sticky tape (Warm Up)
- Pens/pencils
- Glue
- A4 and A5 paper
- Toolboxes
- **My Goals** sheets
- Black card (for **Worry Box Template**)
- Foam sheet/card
- Hula hoop
- **Creatures A and B Pictures**
- **Creature A Backstory Board**
- **Creature B Backstory Board**
- **Creature Scenario Table** sheet
- **Worry Box Template**
- **Hug Tree Template**
- Emotion cards and envelopes
- **Emotion Faces** sheet
- **Emotions Change Card**

TEACHING INPUT OVERVIEW

1. Warm Up: wrist-tied exercise – wrapping a parcel.
2. Recap Rules and Workshop 3 Content.
3. List risk and protective factors – personality, social, school, family (safety and vulnerability).
4. Adding strategies to emotion envelopes – share.
5. Testing, stopping and throwing away negative thoughts.
6. Loop de Loop Teamwork.

Warm Up: Parcel Wrap (15 minutes)

Resources

- Empty shoe box
- String/fabric strips
- Scissors
- Wrapping paper
- Sticky tape

Organise the students to sit in an inward-facing circle. Ask them first to work in pairs and hold out their arms to the side and tie themselves together to their neighbour around the wrist using the string/material. Wrists should be tied firmly but loose enough to be comfortable. They then repeat this as pairs with the person on the opposite side. (5 minutes)

The whole group should now be connected and 'all tied up'. The goal is to use the resources in the middle of the table to wrap a present together. They have 10 minutes to complete the task. Before starting the challenge, tell students not to pull or drag each other as this can result in injuries.

Recap Rules and Workshop 3 Content (5 minutes)

Resources

- Toolboxes

- **My Goals** sheets (from previous workshops)

Have the contents of one person's toolbox in front of you and ask the students about what they remember from last week. Talk through how to use each tool and that we will be looking at some more strategies today.

Ask students to write where they are on their **My Goals** sheet. It might be the same as or different to last week.

Risk and Protective Factors (20 minutes)

Resources

- Copies of **Creatures A and B Pictures**

- Copies of **Creature A Backstory Board**

- Copies of **Creature B Backstory Board**

- Copies of **Creature Scenario Table**

- Pens/pencils

Explain to the children that we are now going to look at what things in people's lives might make it harder or easier for them to cope. We will look at three areas of life – Personality, Family, and Social and Environment.

Split the group in half and assign one half A and the other B. Give the students a picture of their creature: A or B (from the **Creatures A and B Pictures** sheet).

Tell Teams A and B they have 1 minute to come up with names for their creature. Ask them to write their chosen name on their sheet.

Now split each team into two again.

Give each sub-group their relevant **Creature Backstory Board** sheet (A/B) and ask the students to complete the **Creature Scenario Table** resource (personality, social and environment, family) using the information about their creature's life.

Go through the questions on the **Creature Scenario Table** sheet together as a class, writing each group's answers on the board under the headings 'Risk factors' and 'Protective factors'. Reflect on what things might be difficult in some people's lives and what help is available to everybody.

Resource: Creatures A and B Pictures

Resource: Creature A Backstory Board

Social

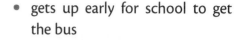

- lives in a little old house a long way from school

- the house needs some repairs and is cold

- has small meals because food is expensive, and is often hungry

- doesn't play out much as the area isn't verv safe

- gets up early for school to get the bus

- finds school hard and doesn't talk to teachers much

- has a support teacher that helps them in class

- has two good friends and enjoys playing with them

- one friend does silly things and often gets injured

- one friend is a bit sad sometimes

Personality

- mostly happy and helpful

- finds words hard because of dyslexia

- gets nervous about new things

- is sometimes not very confident and a bit shy

Family

- lives with dad, sister and pet

- looks after dad who is in a wheelchair – makes meals and helps do the shopping

- the family is very loving and calm

Resource: Creature B Backstory Board

Social

- lives in a big warm house near school

- has a big back garden and lots of space

- has a good neighbourhood

- has lots of parks nearby

- goes to the parks with family some weekends and is allowed to go on their own sometimes

- is good at schoolwork

- sometimes gets told off for talking

- teachers expect them to always do well

- has lots of friends at school but doesn't see them outside of school because of chess competitions

- sometimes gets into arguments with friends

Personality

- is confident and likes talking to others

- is very able and clever

- sometimes does things without thinking, like jumping into other people's games, and gets into arguments often

Family

- lives with foster family: mum, dad, two brothers and sister

- misses their real family but is happy and feels safe

- foster mum and dad encourage them to play chess – they expect them to practise a lot and take them to competitions

Resource: Creature Scenario Table

	Things that are difficult in your creature's life	Things that are good in your creature's life
Personality		
Family		
Social and Environment		
House Neighbourhood School Friends		

Who can your creature ask for help with their homework? What might stop them asking for help?

....

....

What things might stop your creature concentrating in class?

....

....

What things might stop your creature doing things they want to?

....

....

What are your creature's strengths?

....

....

Who are the people in your creature's life that can help it?

....

....

Worry Box (10 minutes)

Resources

- **Worry Box Template** made of black card (one per student)

- Glue

- A4 paper

- Pens/pencils

Tell the students we are going to make a 'worry box' so that when we have worrying thoughts that go round and round in our heads we can write them down and post them in the box. This way they go away or we can come back to them later if we need to.

Give each student a **Worry Box Template** and walk through gluing the sides together as you demonstrate with your box. Then say something along these lines:

> *If worries stay in our heads, they can get bigger and we might start to worry about other things too, a bit like a snowball that gathers up more snow as it rolls. If you feel worried CHECK what your worries are and write them down while they are a small lump of snow. Using your A4 paper write down any worries you have had in the past in a list then cut/tear each one out, fold it up and put it in your worry box. Sometimes using our worry box at night can help us put our worries aside and sleep better.*

Resource: Worry Box Template

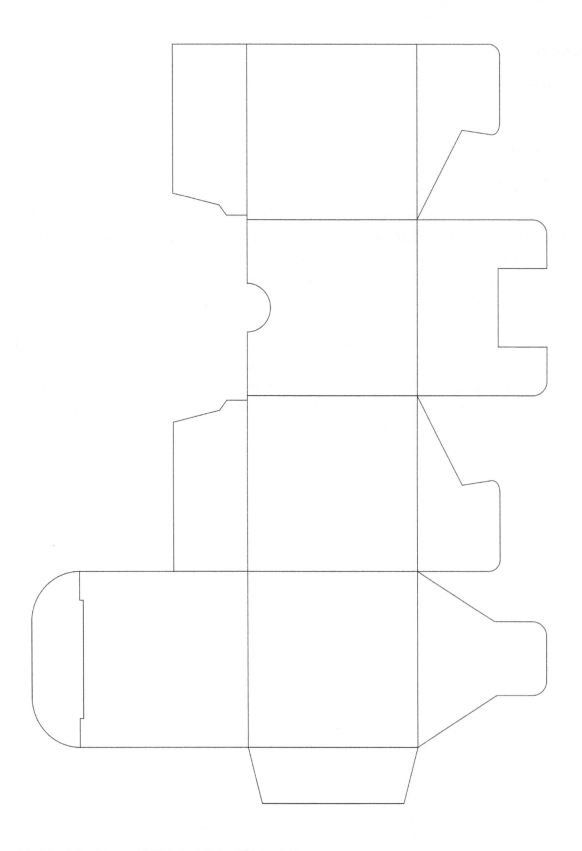

Hug Tree (10 minutes)

Resources

- Pre-prepared foam tree template (branches of different sizes only – no leaves)

- A4 paper

- Pens/pencils

Tell students that sometimes we need a hug – can anyone think of a time they've needed a hug? Give the example of the creature that has a problem it needs to solve as in the scenarios in the Risk and Protective Factors activity. Now give the students the **Hug Tree Template** and ask them to trace around it leaving the picture of a bald tree.

Tell the children that the negative or bad things that are in the creature's head, or its problems, can be written on the branches. Suggest that if it is a big thought they should use a big branch, and for smaller ones a small branch. Next, they draw leaves on each branch with ideas of how to help the creature feel better for each worry/problem branch.

Resource: Hug Tree Template

Identifying Emotions: Emotion Faces (10 minutes)

Resources

- **Emotion Faces** sheet

Hold up the sheet with photographs of people's faces depicting different emotions (**Emotion Faces**). Go through each picture one at a time and ask the students to discuss them. For example, the girl in the bottom right looks overwhelmed: how could she make herself feel better?

Resource: Emotion Faces

Matching Emotions to Tools (47 minutes)

Resources

- Emotion cards
- Envelopes
- **Emotion Faces** sheets
- Sheets of A5 paper
- Pens/pencils
- Glue

Ask the students to collect the emotion envelopes they created in the activity Emotion Role Play and Movement and go through each emotion in turn with them: sad/worried/angry/scared. They then complete the steps below until all emotion envelopes are complete:

- They choose the emotion card they would like to be when they are feeling the emotion on the front, for example for 'angry' they may choose the emotion card 'peaceful'.

- They then find the corresponding picture on the **Emotions Faces** sheet and stick it to the A5 paper.

Above the picture, they write the tools they can use to get them from the emotional state on side one to that on side two, choosing from: Soothing Breathing/Relaxation Exercise/Safe Place Imagery/Attention Placing/Worry Box/Hug Tree/Social Network Constellation.

Using Tools to Change Emotions
Role Play (10 minutes)

Resources

- Emotion cards and envelopes

- **Emotion Change Card** copies

- Pens/pencils

Invite the students to get into pairs and designate one 'actor' and one 'watcher'. Explain that the actors will choose one emotion envelope to role play to their watcher, and the watcher will fill in their **Emotions Change Card**. Emotion envelopes and emotion cards are compared in pairs after the role play. Alternate the role of watcher and actor and complete the steps again.

Ask the actors to choose an emotion envelope and spend a few minutes thinking about how to act out each of the three steps. Tell them you will prompt them as they go for each stage of the emotion envelope:

1. The first emotion picture and actions.

2. The tools they can use to help them.

3. The new emotion and actions.

Give each watcher a copy of the **Emotions Change Card** and explain that as their partner acts out each part, they should write down their guess in each section.

	Actors	Watchers
Stage 1	Emotion 1 and actions	What emotion? What actions?
Stage 2	Tools they can use to help	What tools help?
Stage 3	Emotion 2 and actions	What emotion? What actions?

- Stage 1: Begin the activity by inviting the actors to choose an emotion and act it out. Ask the watchers to write their answers. (1 minute)

- Stage 2: Ask the actors to choose the first tool to help them, then act out how they will use it (30 seconds). Ask the watchers to write down the tool. Ask the actors to choose another tool if there is one and act out using it (30 seconds). Repeat this until all students have chosen the relevant number of tools they need (those choosing one/fewer tool(s) can continue acting with that tool if they wish).

- Stage 3: Ask the actors to act out the emotion they are now in (the second side of the cards they created in the previous activity – Matching Emotions to Tools). Ask the watchers to write their answers. (1 minute)

- In pairs, allow the students to compare the watchers' cards and the actors' envelopes. (1 minute)

- Alternate the role of watcher and actor and complete the steps again.

Resource: Emotions Change Card

Watchers
What emotion?
What actions?
What tools help?
What emotion?
What actions?

Loop de Loop Teamwork (10 minutes)

Resources

- Hula hoop

Ask students to stand in a circle and hold hands. Start one hula hoop hanging over one pair of joined hands. Each person in the circle must pass the hoop over themselves and on to the next person without letting go. Allow the hoop to go around the circle a few times then add another hoop (opposite the current one in the circle) or begin a countdown time in which the hoop must complete a circuit, reducing the time if the task is completed.

Workshop 5 Plan

Theme Four: Identifying Signature Strengths

1. Key Learning Objectives, Resources and Teaching Input Overview

2. Warm Up: Willow in the Wind Trust Exercise (18 minutes)*

3. Recap Rules and Workshop 4 Content (3 minutes)

4. Strengths (15 minutes)*

5. Belonging and Responsibility (15 minutes)*

6. Emotion Thermometers (35 minutes)*

7. Planning: Making the Most of Things That Are Important (15 minutes)*

8. Helium Cane Teamwork (7 minutes)*

KEY LEARNING OBJECTIVES

- To work on turn taking
- To identify individuals' strengths
- To share and explore the meaning of these strengths and how to utilise them
- To explore sympathy and empathy
- To develop the concept of self-management of emotional wellbeing

RESOURCES

- Toolboxes
- A4 paper and pens/colours
- **My Goals** sheet
- Foam A4 squares/card/lollipop sticks/coloured dot stickers/shapes for Feeling Thermometers
- Strengths cards and stickers (homemade)[1]
- Bamboo or gardening cane
- **Belonging and Responsibility Teacher Prompt** sheet
- **Belonging and Responsibility** worksheet
- **Thermometer Worksheet**
- **Plant Metaphor** worksheet

TEACHING INPUT OVERVIEW

1. Warm Up: Willow in the Wind Trust Exercise. Discuss who to trust.

2. Recap Rules and Workshop 4 Content.

3. Strengths, belonging and responsibility and relationships.

4. Emotion Thermometers.

5. Identifying what is important to me. Planning to make the most of things that are important. Being grateful.

6. Helium Cane – discuss balance.

---

1   Or for example as found on Innovativeresources.org.

Warm Up: Willow in the Wind
Trust Exercise (18 minutes)

The objective of this exercise is to develop trust and improve teamwork through cooperation and support. It is important that you monitor safety closely throughout the exercise.

Brief and Set Up (5 minutes)

Tell the students that this exercise is called Willow in the Wind and is about trust. Organise the group into an inward-facing circle and spread large and small participants evenly to avoid any weak points.

One person in the team is selected to be 'the Willow' and stands in an upright and rigid position in the centre of the circle. On your instruction, the Willow leans into the wind and is gently passed around the circle in any direction by the 'spotters'. The Willow must keep their feet absolutely still at all times and put their trust in the rest of the team. Before you start, demonstrate the spotting technique and Willow stance (as outlined below) emphasising the importance of maintaining this throughout. Ask the students to assume each position with you as a practice:

- spotting technique: one foot in front of the other in a T-shape position, arms outstretched, elbows locked, ready and alert

- the Willow position: feet together, arms crossed with hands on shoulders, body straight and eyes closed.

Ensure spotters are close together in a tight circle, shoulder to shoulder and maintaining the correct spotting positions.

Trust Exercise (10 minutes)

Spotters stand with their hands almost touching the participant in the middle. The Willow is then gently passed around the circle.

Spotters may stand further away when confidence is built. Rotate the participants, allowing all students a turn as the Willow if they choose to.

Discussion (3 minutes)

Talk about how easy/hard it was to trust the others.

Ask how easy/hard the task was.

Discuss what trust means for everyone in everyday life, both how to trust others and how to be trustworthy for others.

Discuss the meanings of: 'reliable', 'dependable', 'fair', 'loyal', 'consistent'.

Recap Rules and Workshop 4 Content (3 minutes)

Resources

- **My Goals** sheets

- Pens/pencils

Ask students what they can remember and recap on the important features and how to achieve the outcome: Hug Tree/Worry Box/releasing negative thoughts/getting from one emotion to another by choosing different strategies.

Ask students to score their **My Goals** sheets.

Strengths (15 minutes)

Resources

- Strength cards/stickers
- Emotion envelopes
- Pens/pencils

Sit the students in a circle around a table, with the strengths cards spread over it. Ask the students to look at the cards and choose three to five that best describe their strengths.

Ask each student to talk about a strength that they have identified and how it helps them in life. Go around the circle twice.

Now ask the students to think about what strengths could help them when they are feeling sad/angry/worried/scared.

Using a set of stickers, each child should then stick two or three relevant stickers on the back of each emotion envelope, or write the statement if the stickers are not available – for example 'I am reliable', 'I listen', 'I care about others'.

Belonging and Responsibility (15 minutes)

Resources

- Pens/pencils
- **Belonging and Responsibility Teacher Prompt** sheet
- **Belonging and Responsibility** worksheet

Ask students to complete the **Belonging and Responsibility** worksheet, saying something like:

> *We all have positive and negative responsibilities in different areas: to 'do something' and 'not do something'. On the* **Belonging and Responsibility** *worksheet write down the responsibilities you have in each area of your life.*

Prompt as necessary using the **Belonging and Responsibility Teacher Prompt** sheet. Students may converse in pairs or small groups. After they have completed the worksheet, feedback answers as a group.

Resource: Belonging and Responsibility Teacher Prompt

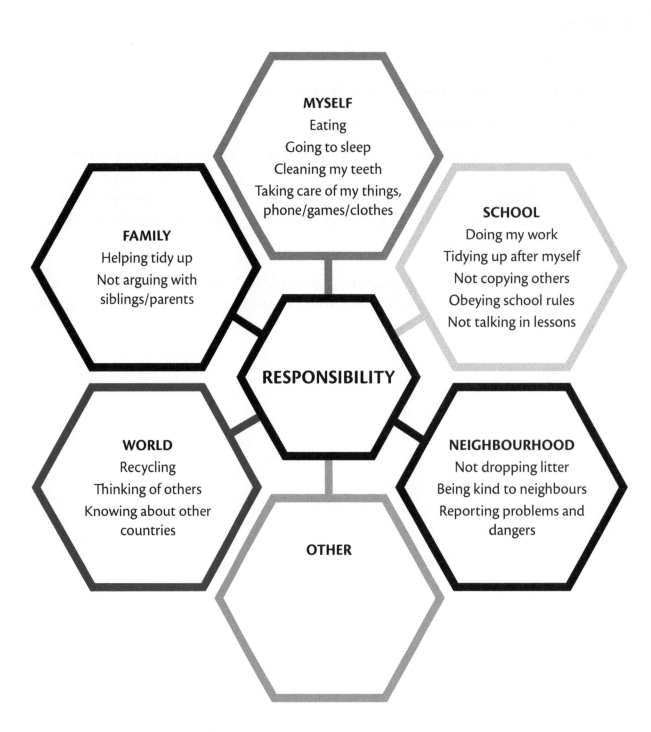

MYSELF
Eating
Going to sleep
Cleaning my teeth
Taking care of my things,
phone/games/clothes

FAMILY
Helping tidy up
Not arguing with
siblings/parents

SCHOOL
Doing my work
Tidying up after myself
Not copying others
Obeying school rules
Not talking in lessons

RESPONSIBILITY

WORLD
Recycling
Thinking of others
Knowing about other
countries

NEIGHBOURHOOD
Not dropping litter
Being kind to neighbours
Reporting problems and
dangers

OTHER

Resource: Belonging and Responsibility

We have positive and negative responsibilities in different areas: 'do something' and 'not do something'. In the areas below write down the responsibilities you have in each area of your life.

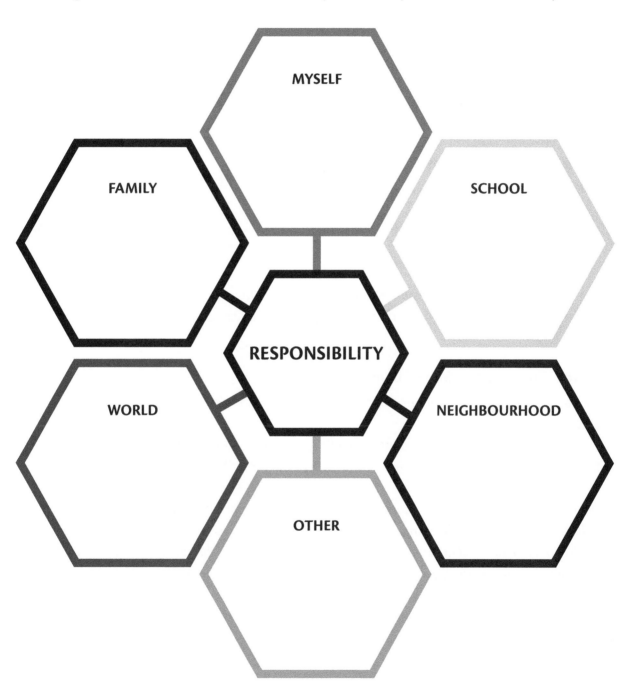

MYSELF

FAMILY

SCHOOL

RESPONSIBILITY

WORLD

NEIGHBOURHOOD

OTHER

Emotion Thermometers (35 minutes)

Resources

- Coloured dot stickers

- Card/foam sheets

- Lollipop sticks

- **Thermometer Worksheet** (copy for each student)

Making Emotion Thermometers (25 minutes)

Introduce the first part of the activity to the children:

> We will be looking at how fluid moods are and how feelings can change – sometimes slowly and sometimes quickly.

Using the **Thermometer Worksheet** and craft items, allow the students to make their own thermometer with the degrees of strength clearly labelled on the side.

Emotion Thermometer Story (10 minutes)

Now pair the students up and give each pair a different emotion to measure during the story: happy/angry/sad/worried.

Tell the students that you are going to read them a story about a character called Ahmed and that they will be thinking about the different phases of Ahmed's emotions. Then say:

> While I am reading the story about Ahmed, use the dot stickers to mark on the thermometer where you think Ahmed's feelings are up to. What increases and decreases during the story?
>
> When Ahmed is feeling your emotion during the story move, the sticky spot as you think his emotions might change. If you make a change, hold up your thermometer.

Throughout the story notice when thermometers are held up and acknowledge the students' input.

> Ahmed has been out in the school yard at break time. There will be an activity in the hall next so Ahmed returns to the classroom and goes to his tray to get his favourite pencil and rubber to start the lesson. When he opens his tray, he can't see his favourite poop emoji rubber and

Minion pencil. When he reaches to the back, instead of finding his rubber and pencil he finds a broken pencil and a dirty white rubber with teeth marks in it. What might Ahmed think?

Because everyone is rushing to get to the activity in the hall, Ahmed can't see the class teacher or his best friends. He picks up the broken pencil and dirty rubber and sits in the corner of the classroom. His teacher asks Ahmed to come into the hall. How might Ahmed respond?

In the hall the activities are starting so Ahmed goes and sits at the back. As he looks up, he sees the new classroom helper walking past with his rubber and pencil and rushes over.

Through discussion, draw out how many times the students moved the sticker on their thermometer and how emotions can change – sometimes quickly, sometimes slowly.

Resource: Thermometer Worksheet

My Feeling Thermometer

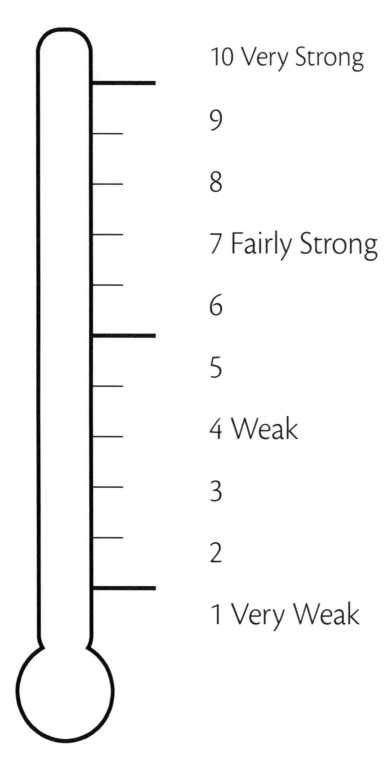

10 Very Strong

9

8

7 Fairly Strong

6

5

4 Weak

3

2

1 Very Weak

Planning: Making the Most of Things That Are Important (15 minutes)

Resources

- **Plant Metaphor** worksheet

- Pens/pencils

Give students the **Plant Metaphor** worksheet and explain:

> *Imagine you are this plant. Draw on it all the things that will help you grow happy and healthy. You can fill it in however you like but here are some examples:*
>
> - ***Keep me strong and healthy*** *(stem/trunk = what I can do, e.g. be positive, healthy)*
>
> - ***Bring me sunshine*** *(environment = things I enjoy doing and people that make me happy)*
>
> - ***Feed me*** *(roots = good relationships and things I need: food, sleep, exercise, love)*
>
> - ***Prickly weeds and leaf-eating bugs*** *= avoid things that attack us or stop us being able to grow properly, e.g. worry, bad friendships, pressures*
>
> - ***Petals and leaves*** *= your strengths and skills*

Resource: Plant Metaphor

Draw your own plant on a piece of paper...

Helium Cane Teamwork (7 minutes)

Resources

* Bamboo/gardening cane

Split the group in two and ask the students to stand facing each other (a line of pairs). Introduce the bamboo cane. Ask students to hold their arms out in front of them and point their index fingers, lay the cane across their extended index fingers and allow everyone to adjust so that the cane is horizontal and the cane is resting horizontally along their fingers.

Explain that the task is for each pair in turn to lower the cane to the ground without fingers losing contact with it. Everyone's finger must remain in contact with the cane and it must rest on top of the fingers only – no holding or pinching the cane to steady it.

Every time a finger loses contact, the task will be restarted.

This activity is designed to demonstrate the importance and advantages of working with other people who want to help you to achieve good mental health. Giving help to and accepting support from others can help you to achieve better balance in your life.

Theme Five: Using Signature Strengths and Support Networks and Post-Intervention Assessment

1. Key Learning Objectives, Resources and Teaching Input Overview

2. Warm Up: Problem Solving (20 minutes)*

3. Recap Rules and Workshops 1–5 Content (15 minutes)

4. Getting Rid of Negative Thoughts: Balloons (15 minutes)*

5. Mentally Healthy Poster (40 minutes)*

6. Voice Interviews and Quiz (20 minutes)

7. Post-Intervention Assessment and Certificate Presentation (20 minutes)

KEY LEARNING OBJECTIVES

- To understand what our particular strengths are and how to utilise them in difficult times
- To identify who is in our support network and how to find other sources of support
- To recap on learning from Workshops 1–5

RESOURCES

- Files/toolboxes (as appropriate to age and stage)
- A3/4 paper and coloured pens/pencils
- Dictation App/Dictaphones (for qualitative outcome questions)
- Post-intervention Assessment Tools
- **My Goals** sheets
- Balloons (prepared as directed)
- Old magazines
- **Brain Teasers** (sheets **1**, **2**, **3** and **Answers**)
- **Certificate**

TEACHING INPUT OVERVIEW

1. Warm Up – brain teasers.
2. Recap Rules and Workshops 1–5 Content.
3. Getting Rid of Negative Thoughts (balloons activity).
4. Create a Mentally Healthy Poster.
5. Voice Interviews in pairs with agreed questions.
6. Mental Health quiz.
7. Repeat completion of the pre-intervention outcome and wellbeing measures from the Assessment Tools in Workshop 1 as a post-intervention assessment exercise to measure progress.
8. Present certificates.

Warm Up: Problem Solving (20 minutes)

Resources

- Copies of **Brain Teasers** (**1**, **2** and **3**)

- Pens/pencils

Give out the **Brain Teasers** sheet(s) and ask the group to work as two teams to solve the problems. They should work down the list for as many as you have time for.

Resource: Brain Teasers 1

Annie is the world's strongest woman. She has won this title five years in a row – yet there is one thing that weighs virtually nothing that she finds impossible to hold for more than a minute. What is it?

Which of these two timekeepers has the most moving parts?

The space voyager, Stargazer, crashed into an unknown planet on its first-ever flight. The planet was made of the strongest rock known to man. Where did they bury the survivors?

Resource: Brain Teasers 2

On a warm morning in springtime Cheryl is walking down the road and finds two lumps of coal and a carrot on the pavement. How did they get there?

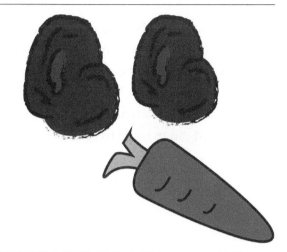

What is so delicate that if you say it out loud you break it?

How many times can you take 6 away from 36?

Jeff the monkey had been walking all day and was extremely thirsty when he noticed a hole in the ground with a pile of rocks at the side of it. He was amazed when he found that the hole had water in the bottom, but as he looked down he thought, 'I'll never reach that!' But Jeff did manage to reach the water. How did he do it?

Ruby brings a newspaper to Mr Powell every day of the week and even at the weekend. Mr Powell never pays Ruby. Why does she do this?

How is it possible to throw a ball in one direction and have it come straight back to you?

Resource: Brain Teasers Answers

Annie cannot hold her breath for more than a minute.

The egg timer has thousands of grains of moving sand.

You cannot bury survivors.

It is early spring and the sun has melted a snowman.

Silence.

Once. If you take six away a second time you take it away from 30 not 36.

Jeff puts the rocks in the hole so the water rises to the top so he can drink it.

Ruby is Mr Powell's dog.

Throw the ball *up.*

Recap Rules and Workshops 1–5
Content (15 minutes)

Resources

- Toolbox and contents

In order to revise and evaluate what participants have learned during the workshops, lay out one toolbox and each of the resources contained within it that have been used or created during each session. Ask each participant one by one, to describe one of the worksheets or resources and what they learned from that activity.

Reinforce the Mind Mechanics™ job of NOTICE, CHECK and CHANGE as explained in the Attention Cycle activity in Workshop 3.

Getting Rid of Negative Thoughts: Balloons (15 minutes)

Resources

- Balloons (two per student)
- Pens suitable for writing on balloons

How to get rid of negative thoughts and hold on to positive thoughts

Explain to the students that thoughts are simply that: an idea we have constructed or remembered and which floats around our head. A thought is not a fact. To demonstrate this give each participant a balloon and assist them to blow it up but not tie it. Help each person to write a negative adjective on their balloon to describe themselves. Then encourage the student to let go of the balloon and enjoy the funny sound and sight of it deflating and whizzing around the room. Explain that we can let go of negative thoughts in our heads in a similar way.

Now give each person a balloon and ask that they blow it up and tie a knot, helping them as needed. This time they write a positive thought about themselves or about another member of the group and hold onto the balloon or bat it to their friend. In this way they are encouraged to hold onto positive thoughts to soothe themselves.

Mentally Healthy Poster (40 minutes)

Resources

- A1/2/3 paper

- Art materials (minimum coloured pencils)

- Magazines

Tell the students they are going to create a poster individually or in pairs for the school to help everyone stay healthy and happy. As Mind Mechanics™ they write down on the paper and draw the people that can help if they need support with problems at home, at school or at clubs.

They should then add all the things that can help them to be mentally healthy – any strategies, any physical things (exercise, eating well, sleeping regularly) – using all the things they have learnt.

Voice Interviews and Quiz (20 minutes)

Resources

- Dictaphones/voice recording app

- Paper

- Pens/pencils

Ask the students to get into pairs. They then take it in turn to use the voice recording app/dictaphone to ask each other questions based on what they have learned about self-regulating their mental health during Mind Mechanics™. Model what is and isn't appropriate to say and spend a little time explaining that we may use these recordings to share our newfound expertise with other students or teachers or parents, so we might not want to give very personal specific answers. For example, it might be fine to say, 'Now when I get angry, instead of kicking my chair I use my breathing,' but you might not want to say someone's name; for example, 'When Joe is being mean and making me cry, I distract myself and get busy with one of the activities I love to do'.

Ask the same pairs to create a mental health quiz based on all the things they have learned. Ask them to come up with 10 questions (either direct or multiple choice) in teams. The students then get into two teams, each team combining the questions generated by the pairs, to play the quiz.

Post-Intervention Assessment and Certificate Presentation (20 minutes)

Ask the participants to complete the same assessment sheets as they did pre-assessment (see Workshop 1's photocopiable/downloadable resources), this time in a different colour. Discuss their progress. Use this data to promote the programme in your setting and to flag up students who may need professional intervention. (15 minutes)

Present the group with their certificates. Plan an assembly for the newly qualified Mind Mechanics™ to share their learning. (5 minutes)

CONGRATULATIONS

_____

You have made a fantastic contribution to

MIND MECHANICS™

Thank you for being an excellent student

Mind Mechanics

Impact Data and Case Study

OUTCOME MEASURE DATA AIM

To find out what impact the Mind Mechanics™ Workshops have on young people's emotional literacy, self-regulation and interpersonal functioning alongside their overall feelings towards themselves and their lives.

Method

We collected data using four methods: three self-report questionnaires/scales and a set of open questions about students' experience of the workshops. The following three measures were taken at the beginning of the first workshop and the end of the last workshop.

Me and My Life Assessment Rating Scale
The rating scale asked students to rate how proficient they were in the following areas using a scale of 0 (not good) to 10 (very good):

- being able to keep positive relationships

- being able to understand their/other people's feelings

- how good they feel about themselves

- how excited they feel about their future

- being able to show/tell other people how they are feeling

- how well they can calm themselves down

- being able to overcome difficult situations.

Emotion tick boxes
Students were presented with a pictorial display of emotions and asked to choose those that they could relate to how they were feeling in that moment. They could pick as

many or as few as they wished. The seven emotions in bold were processed as positive emotions and the eleven that are underlined were processed as negative. The remaining two were neutral and not calculated:

Confident	Okay	Hurt	Happy
Angry	Stressed	Tired	Grieving
Calm	Optimistic	Anxious	Positive
Irritable	Guilty	Sad	Disappointed
Excited	Lonely	Shy	Withdrawn

Life rating scale pole

A life rating scale asked students to show where they felt they were on a continuum, with the bottom being not very good to the top being good. This was in relation to:

- how they feel (not very good to fantastic)

- whether they would like to change things in their life or if they are happy as they are

- feeling negative or positive about things in their life

- liking or not liking themselves.

Qualitative open-ended questions

At the end of the workshops the following questions were asked to the students in pairs:

- What have you learnt during these workshops?

- Is there anything you've learnt about yourself or other people or your emotions?

- What do you think of all the strategies in your toolbox?

- What would you like to learn more about?

- How might you support yourself through difficult times and emotions?

- How might you help others with what you have learnt?

Whole group data

The figures below show whole group pre- and post-intervention scores alongside the percentage change for each measure for participants.

Seven star rating scale

The biggest increases in capacity for the students who took part as a group (with a percentage change above 25 per cent) were in their ability to:

- calm themselves down

- understand their own and others' feelings

- keep positive relationships

- feel good about themselves.

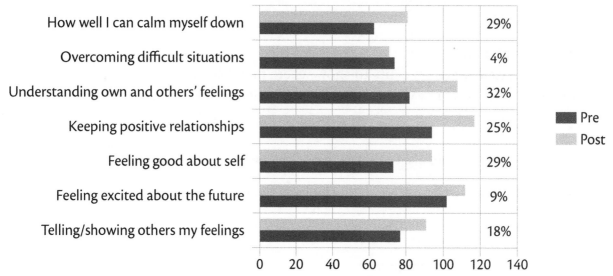

Figure A1 Seven star rating scale scores

Emotion tick boxes

In the reporting of positive and negative emotions pre- and post-Mind Mechanics™ relating to how students feel 'at this moment about life in general' the figures below show an 81 per cent increase in the reporting of positive emotions and a 39 per cent decrease in the reporting of negative emotions.

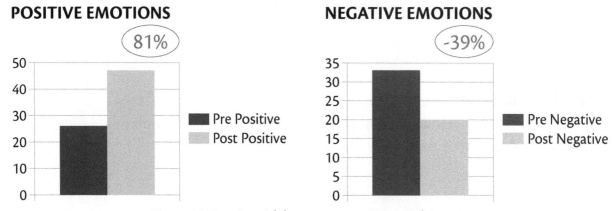

Figure A2 Emotion tick boxes scores: positive and negative

Life rating scale pole

This figure shows the whole group pre- and post-intervention scores and percentage change for how they perceive themselves and lives at this current moment. The biggest percentage change related to the reporting of feeling happy about life.

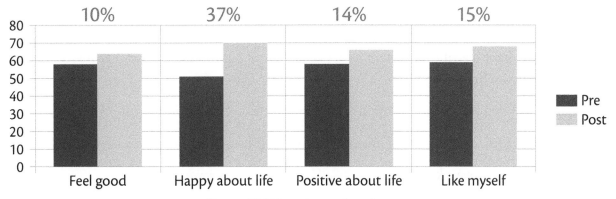

Figure A3 Life rating scale pole scores

The table below shows the percentage increase/decrease of self-reported movement on each question from the three measures for the total cohort participating in pilots and evaluations. These figures were calculated by collating the individual scores of the students who completed pre- and post-intervention measures, finding the percentage increase/decrease for them as a group.

Measure	Question data	Percentage increase/ decrease minus anomaly
Seven star rating scale	Telling/showing others my feelings	20.69
	Feeling excited about the future	28.21
	Feeling good about self	73.08
	Keeping positive relationships	21.43
	Understanding own and others' feelings	80.77
	Overcoming difficult situations	0.00
	How well I can calm myself down	21.43
Emotion tick boxes	Increase in positive emotions	58.33
	Decrease of negative emotions	62.50
Life rating scale pole	Feeling good	15.15
	Happy about life	58.33
	Positive about life	20.00
	Liking myself	25.00

Qualitative open-ended questions

What have you learnt during these workshops?

Student 1: So much nice things. I've learnt to be more surrounded by my friends and I like being around my mum, dad and all my relatives. I enjoy it a lot more now.

I've learnt how to basically act around other people because I used to, like, hurt other people but now I don't, I like hugging them.

Student 2: I have learnt that to help with my anger I can use the stress ball, the memories, I can use the breathing buddy.

Student 3: When you get angry I didn't know you could use relaxation to calm you down.

Student 4: How to control your anger by using your breathing buddy and stress ball.

Is there anything you've learnt about yourself or other people or your emotions?

Student 2: That I can trust some people.

What do you think of all the strategies in your toolbox?

Student 5: Great.

Student 6: I think the breathing buddy is my favourite and I will probably use it the most.

Student 7: I liked the memory jar, every single colour was a memory. I feel happy when I look at it, it can help to not forget memories.

I will use my stress ball when I'm angry by squeezing it.

CASE STUDY

Following intervention, we compared pre- with post-intervention scales in order to demonstrate the measure of change.

Here we present a case study for one boy who engaged with this intervention. The goals of the intervention were to offer structure and a therapeutic toolbox to provide containment and consistency to enable Ben to self-regulate his emotional wellbeing.[1]

Ben's outcome scores were significantly positive post-intervention, as you will see from the outcome data measure below.

Ben

Ben is nine years old. In the pre-intervention discussion, he was described as having a comorbid autism spectrum condition (ASC) and ADHD diagnosis. Ben is in foster care and had been defined as a Child in Need.

---

1 His name has been anonymised to allow for confidentiality.

He was feeling very angry towards his mother and was engaged with Child and Adult Mental Health Services (CAMHS). He had low self-esteem and behavioural issues and felt significantly negative about himself.

Ben engaged well with the workshops and looked forward to attending the sessions.

When asked what he had learnt from the workshops, Ben said: 'I have learnt that to help with my anger, I can use my stress ball, the breathing buddy and the memory jar.'

When asked whether there was anything he'd learnt about himself, other people or his emotions, he replied: 'That I can now trust some people.'

Feedback from Ben's teacher was that he had benefitted hugely from group sessions and she described how his therapeutic toolkit had become part of his provision and he was successfully using the toolkit as a coping mechanism. She reported that Ben was talking more openly about his feelings and that he was now engaging significantly better in forming friendships within class. She, and also other staff members, had noticed a significant change in his self-esteem, specifically in that there had been a significant reduction in him feeling and expressing negative emotions about himself.

The following figures clearly demonstrate the success of the intervention. Using the full range of assessment tools provides a different range of responses and movement, which is captured across the three charts.

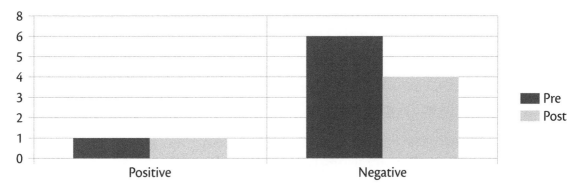

Figure A4 Movement of positive and negative emotions snapshot

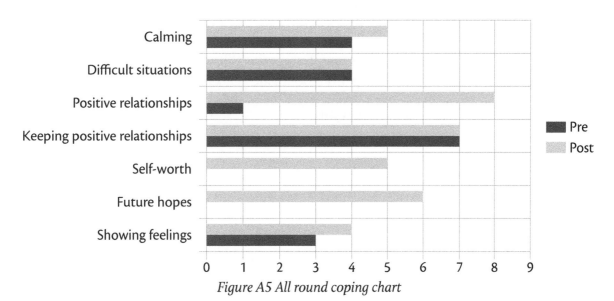

Figure A5 All round coping chart

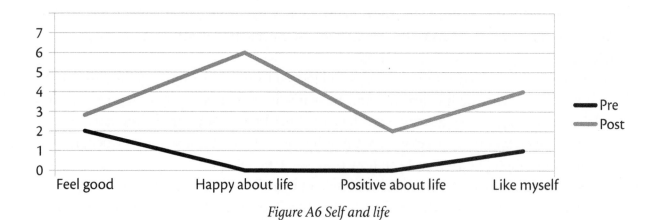

Figure A6 Self and life

Feedback from school personnel

- School personnel reported finding the Mind Mechanics™ resources, wording and vocabulary to be effective and accurate in terms of emotional literacy. They found the resources flexible and adaptable.

- They felt the workshops, with some adaptation, would benefit younger students.

- Students who attended the pilot scheme are still managing to pay fewer visits to the Inclusion Resource Centre. They are making better choices, even though for most of the cohorts their home situation hasn't changed.

- Students really benefitted from the workshops by applying their toolkits to difficult situations, thus building self-esteem.

- Students enjoyed and looked forward to attending the workshops even though, for some of them, this meant missing their favourite lessons.

- Parents were really on board with the workshops and there were no refusals for their children to attend. They reported positive changes in their child's behaviour.

- Some of the parents attended a meeting where staff introduced the Mind Mechanics™ programme and demonstrated a mindfulness resource, which the parents found to be a useful therapeutic tool to aid relaxation.

- No negative impacts were reported at all.